SEWING CLOTHES KiDS LOVE

Creative Publishing
international

First published in the United States of America by
Creative Publishing international, Inc., a member of
Quayside Publishing Group
400 First Avenue North
Suite 300
Minneapolis, MN 55401
1-800-328-3895
www.creativepub.com
Visit www.Craftside.Typepad.com for a behind-the-scenes peek at our crafty world!

ISBN-13: 978-1-58923-473-4
ISBN-10: 1-58923-473-1

10 9 8 7 6 5 4 3 2 1

Library of Congress Cataloging-in-Publication Data

Langdon, Nancy J. S.
  Sewing clothes kids love : sewing patterns and instructions for boys and girls outfits / Nancy J.S. Langdon and Sabine Pollehn.
      p. cm.
  Includes index.
  ISBN-13: 978-1-58923-473-4
  ISBN-10: 1-58923-473-1
1. Children's clothing. I. Pollehn, Sabine. II. Title.

TT635.L35 2010
646.4'06--dc22

2009031409

Technical Editors: Carol Fresia and Carol Spier
Copy Editor: Nancy Chute
Proofreader: Karen Levy
Book Design: Kathie Alexander
Cover Design: Kathie Alexander
Illustrations: Mario Ferro
Pattern Drafter: Anja Müssig
Photographs: Nancy J. S. Langdon

Printed in China

NANCY J.S. LANGDON AND SABINE POLLEHN

SEWING CLOTHES KIDS LOVE

SEWING PATTERNS AND INSTRUCTIONS
FOR BOYS' AND GIRLS' OUTFITS

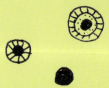

This book is dedicated to my daughter, Anna. You sparkle and shine and light up my world.

Acknowledgments

I didn't write this book alone and, in many ways, I did not make the clothes for my kids all by myself. I learned a trick and technique here and there. I gleaned inspiration from so many. I used the fabrics and notions designed by some wonderful artisans. I hope I will be able to share with you a good deal of what has been shared with me. It has been my great privilege to collaborate with creative minds around the world in a spirit of friendship and fun.

This book would not have been possible without the generous contributions of many people. I would like to acknowledge my great debt to editor Deborah Cannarella, editor John Gettings, publisher Winnie Prentiss, and team at Creative Publishing international for their faith in me and the enthusiasm for our work. My very special thanks to technical editors Carol Spier and Carol Fresia for sharing their knowledge and ideas and for their care with the manuscript.

I wish to extend my deep gratitude to the following: to my beautiful models and their families, Chase, Kristin, Amanda, Brooks, Makenna, Kaitlyn, Samantha, Regan, Karis, Cayleigh, Brooklynne, Kennedy, Piper, Jack, and Anna; to Anja Müssig for her stunning talent, attention to detail and superb skill in design and drafting; to Melissa Milne for advice on plus-size sewing for kids; to Barbara Bode, Eva Soysal, Diana van Helvoort, Nicole Schmitz, Shan Shan, "Hand Over Fist," Emma Trollman, Sara Shorter, and Toni Hamel for allowing their handiwork to be included; to Pamela Erny for allowing her tear-away tracing technique to be included; to Nicole Hildebrandt, Maiga Dibbern, and Anja "Maki" Brinkmann for allowing their graphic designs to be used in embroideries and notions in the design examples; to Sabine "Creabine" Kesting for her beautiful appliqué examples; to Karen Rennie for assistance with photography; to Jeanette Potthast and Sonja Wintersdorf for embroidery design and technical support; to Chris Fischer for her support and encouragement; to Frieda Mayr for the beautiful appliqué example; to Christoph for his forbearance; and to Janina Pollehn for her indefatigueable positive attitude and contribution to our work.

To contributing editor Sabine Pollehn: thank you. Thank you for all you have done to revive the craft of sewing and for allowing me the opportunity to inspire others, the way you have inspired me.

And to my late mother, Marilyn Langdon, thank you for making the light blue dress with the white pinafore for my three-year-old portrait, my fringy flapper dress Halloween costume in second grade, my velvet and taffeta high school formal dress, the jean jacket I traipsed about in during my high school exchange year, and the black suit I wore to my first job interview.

Nancy

Contents

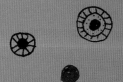

Introduction

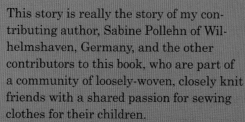

This story is really the story of my contributing author, Sabine Pollehn of Wilhelmshaven, Germany, and the other contributors to this book, who are part of a community of loosely-woven, closely knit friends with a shared passion for sewing clothes for their children.

More than twenty years ago, when Sabine had her first daughter, Janina, she and her husband did not have much money left at the end of the month to buy children's clothes. But she did have a hand-me-down sewing machine and a bit of sewing knowledge learned from her mother and grandmother. Sabine read the local classified ads to find people who were giving away the brightly colored corduroy pants popular at the time. She cut up these old clothes to create a rainbow wardrobe for her daughter. These outfits, which stopped passersby in their tracks, are how Sabine received her first orders to sew one-of-a-kind clothes.

Years later, the World Wide Web came on the scene, and Sabine had two teenage sons with a hankering for html. She began posting images, ideas, and techniques to share with the few people she thought might be interested in sewing children's clothing. Little did she expect the incredible response to her simple website and online gallery. Soon, the klickundblick.de ("click and look") gallery became Europe's number-one site for sewing children's clothes.

Sabine sought out the aid of a couture pattern drafter, Anja Müssig, to draft a pattern or two of her designs. Sabine's email box quickly filled up with requests for copies of the patterns. The demand became too much for this mother of five, so her daughter Janina, who had just earned her business degree, decided to create a small online shop called Farbenmix. The company now has more than 100 sewing patterns, and Farbenmix woven tapes have become a worldwide sensation.

• My online threaded-needle friends Eva Soyal and Barbara Bode collaborated on this dress. Eva knit and crocheted the top, and Barbara sewed the perfect skirt—making the whole much more than the sum of its parts.

The German word *Farbenmix* means "color mix" and reflects Sabine's belief that children want and deserve color, whimsy, and imagination in their world. In addition to sharing her own designs through Farbenmix, Sabine has invited other independent designers and graphic artists into the fold including Anja "Maki" Brinkmann, Maiga Dibbern, Claudia Greb, Nicole Hildebrandt, Sabine "Smila" Kortman, Margaretha "Glitzerblume" Lecher, Dana Lübke, Sandra "Sanna" Moser, Ingrid Nußbaum, Jeanette Potthast, and Eva Soyal. Sabine also invited me, thousands of miles away and on another continent, to share my unconventional sewing and design ideas with the world. Farbenmix is currently distributed throughout North America, Europe, and Australia.

My small business, Studio Tantrum/Fledge, has helped me spread my wings, test the winds, and make a few nervous and occasionally successful leaps from my little perch. The word *fledge* means "capable of flying." I hope that my designs encourage others to take chances with their own creativity.

I like to think of myself as the tap dancer. I say tap dancer because the German verb for "to stitch," *steppen*, is also the verb for "to tap dance." When sewing instructions are translated from German into English by a computer program, they often instruct the sewer to "tap dance." I see it as part of my work to translate this unique approach to sewing for children for the rest of the world to understand and enjoy. Tap dancing is optional.

Chapter 1

Sewing for Children

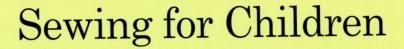

Because childhood is here and gone so quickly, to me it is important to dress a child for each special occasion.

This book contains clothes for all types of special occasions—the conquest of the monkey bars, mastery of a two-wheeled bike, an evening eating ice cream in bed while watching a movie. These are clothes to wear to school, the playground, a playdate, a birthday party, through the puddles, up the trees, and among the weeds and wildflowers. They can be washed and worn and washed and worn again. These are real clothes for real kids. In our opinion, every event in childhood is a special occasion, and every day is a reason to celebrate and a reason to wear special clothes.

Perhaps this book caught your eye because of the many wonderful clothing designs. My hope is that this book will encourage you to try something you haven't done before and for you to make beautiful things for the little ones in your life. But more than that, my goal is for you to have fun. Enjoy!

SEW WITH THE FLOW

When working on a project, you are absorbed in what you are doing. Your focus and attention are on the very next step, the very next seam. Throughout the process, the goal—the final garment—is clear in your mind. This is how action and awareness merge. This is the phenomenon known as flow.

In his book *Flow: The Psychology of Optimal Experience*, author Mihály Csíkszentmihályi defines his concept of flow as having the following characteristics. How I think this can apply to sewing follows in parentheses.

- **Clear goals.** (This is when I have fabric in one hand and a pattern in the other, and I know where I want to go.)

- **Concentration and focusing deeply in an activity.** (Sewing requires accuracy. Garment construction requires an ability to think in three dimensions.)

- **A loss of the feeling of self and self-consciousness.** (Csíkszentmihályi calls it a merging of awareness and action. Judging from the piles of fabrics lying on my floor, I am not very self-conscious about the tidiness of my work space, but I am very focused on the work.)

- **A distorted sense of time.** (Einstein was right: time is relative. Hours seem to go by in the space of minutes when I'm in the sew flow.)

- **Immediate feedback.** (I know right away when a piece is coming together, and I know when to grab the seam ripper.)

- **Walking a line between ability and challenge.** (My projects are never too difficult, and never too easy. I use a pattern as a map, but will easily allow myself to stray from the design to find a new destination.)

- **A sense of control over the situation.** (As I make the garment, I'm in the driver's seat. I control the colors, the fit, and the details. If I drive off the road, a seam ripper is as good as a tow truck to pull me back on track.)

- **The activity is rewarding in itself.** (I find great joy in finding the right combinations in my tangle of colors and textures. And my kids get some new clothes, too.)

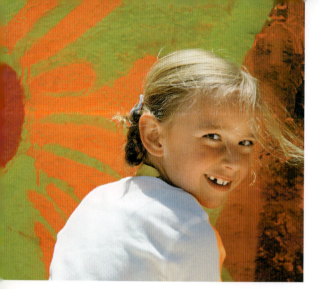

Sewing, Clothes, Kids, and Love

Why sew for your kids? There are many possible answers. These are a few of the best answers I've heard from sewing friends: "I sew because my daughter is so special to me, I want to show it in the clothes she's wearing." "I sew because I love to hear 'You made this? You're kidding!'" "I sew because starting a new project gives me a twist in the stomach, like falling in love." "I feel that I am sewing love around my daughter's tiny body." "I sew because sewing is who I am." I treasure the moment when I put a garment I made onto my precious little one, like a hug from me she can wear all day, and watch her skip off to school. I want your days to be filled with magic moments like that.

When you sew for your child you have the opportunity to create garments that not only fit your child but also suit his or her personality. Sabine and I begin our designs from the bottom up to develop clothes that accommodate the specific needs of small bodies. We consider the proportions, body types, activities, and energy levels of children. For example, our trousers are cut higher in the back because children sit on the floor, squat on their haunches, crawl on all fours, climb trees, and wrestle on the lawn. These normal kid activities can pull down the seat of the trousers. The direction for each pattern includes a measuring chart so you can adjust the fit to your child's body.

When sewing for your child, you also have the opportunity to engage her in the design of the clothes she wears, making her clothing a real reflection of her personality. Look through magazines and patterns together, go fabric shopping together, and pick out colors, prints, and trims as a team. These shared design sessions could very likely become a lifelong activity for the two of you.

Designed to Grow

"Kids grow out of their clothes so fast!" I hear quite often. Yet, my daughter gets at least two, and even three, years of wear from the clothes made from our patterns. She usually wears them out before she outgrows them. Our patterns are designed to "grow" with the child.

Young children generally grow lengthwise, while their shoulder widths and waist sizes stay about the same for a year or longer. So, as we design, we add sleeves that will look good full-length the first year and somewhere above the wrist the next. We make trouser designs that look good at full length and also, later, at high-water and Capri lengths. Our dresses can also be worn as a tunic top over leggings or jeans. We add a bit of elastic in the right places for growth and fit and we put a little swing in our tops, so that they don't stretch over growing tummies. If you choose good-quality fabrics and flexible styles, your garments will enjoy several years of wear.

Cool vs. Cute

Ruffles, embroidery, appliqué, color, frills, flounces, and flowers: these are the things that convinced me to switch on my sewing machine. But what about the guy in the photo at right? As a baby, he didn't have an opinion about his clothes, but that didn't last very long. From a very early age, he had definite opinions about his clothes—and cute wasn't going to cut it. No choo-choo trains with buttons for wheels, thank you very much. Cool (not meaning "cold," but rather an aesthetic of attitude) is the design threshold for this gnarly little "grommet" (not meaning a rough and knotted metal ring, but a cool young surfer). I do feel a great deal of satisfaction when my daughter, Anna, receives compliments on her handmade clothes, but when Jack's buddies say, "Your mom made that? No way. Dude, that is so tight!" (meaning cool, not ill-fitting), I'm pretty stoked myself.

• You've seen him ponder, pose, and primp in front of the mirror. Boys care a great deal about the clothes they wear, too.

KEEPING IT COOL

To get to cool, you need to start from conventional. Cool is the point at which conventional is recognizable but stands on its head. I begin with a very conservative garment design and then go off the rails from there—subtly, incrementally. A garment can look so good that it's bad, and look so bad that it's good again. By the time this book goes to print, kids' slang expressions will likely have changed, as will the fashions, but these rules of thumb will create timeless one-of-a-kind cool clothing for boys:

Colors

Think of the colors in a landscape: deep green tree canopy, brown river, deep gray tree bark, khaki-colored stones, gray clouds, blue ocean. I include bright colors sparingly, but I don't exclude them: think single orange poppy in a field of moss.

Embellishment

Don't avoid details in boys' clothing. In some respects, because of the limited color palette, the little embellished details are even more important. Try stenciling, reverse appliqué, and topstitching in different threads and colors. When choosing motifs, think about the boy's interests and ambitions. My son, Jack, surfs, skateboards, plays soccer, loves to draw, is great at math, is not so good at social studies, and loves all creatures in nature. Those activities give me plenty to work with.

- *Cool or cute? You might tell him he looks cool—but you'll always know how cute that little dickens really is.*

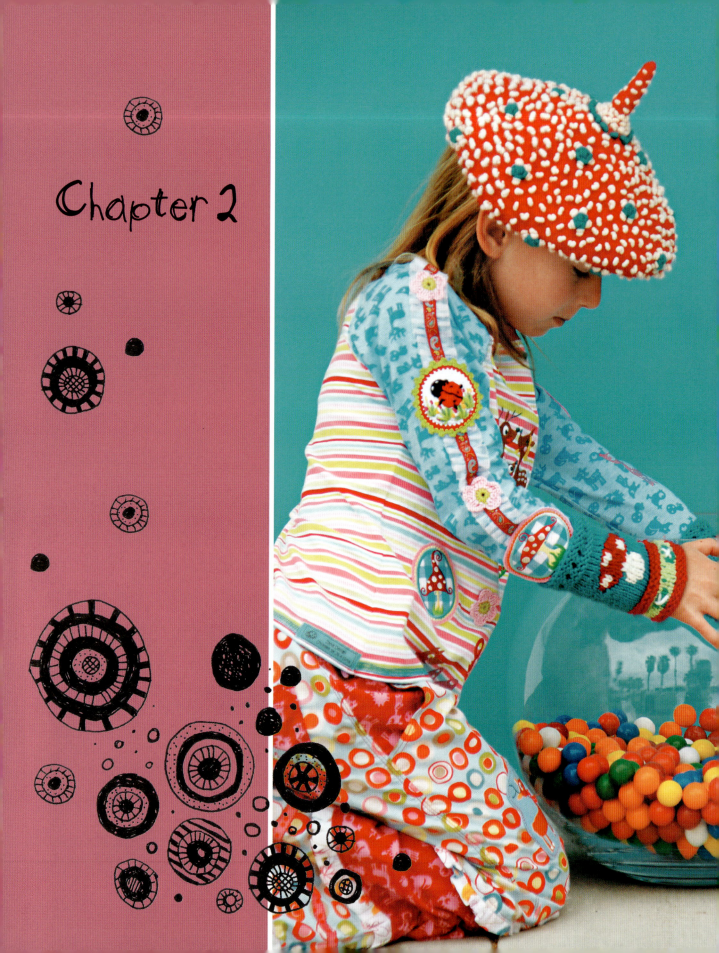

Chapter 2

Color, Fabric, and Gear

One of the really wonderful things about designing for children is the abundance of color and pattern possibilities. As you can see from the designs in this book, Sabine is simply masterful at pulling otherwise disparate fabrics, colors, and trims into a cohesive, whimsical, balanced whole. I often think, "What would Sabine do?" and then reach for a fabric or an embellishment that moves the design in a whole new, exciting direction. Plum and red? Yes! Brown and chartreuse? Yes! Plum and red and brown and chartreuse? Yes!

My personal design choices are based on this idea: Fabrics that do not "match" match when they are sewn together. The seam connecting the fabrics makes all the difference. On the other hand, fabrics that match perfectly may not "match" when they are sewn together. Well, actually, they match too much, and I think lose interest. I think in terms of color volume: Do the fabrics have the same loudness? If so, they will "sound" great together.

Choosing Fabric

Which comes first: the sewing pattern or the fabric? An uncut piece of fabric presents a universe of possibilities; the sewing pattern is the springboard to creativity. Many times, a fabric will "say" exactly what it wants to be. Other times, the shape of the garment will suggest a type of fabric that will produce the ideal form and fit.

Most of the time, I purchase fabric without a specific project in mind. Sabine's number-one rule for fabric shopping is: buy solids, lots and lots of solids. Now, the probability of my purchasing with my head instead of my heart and buying only solids is very slim. Left to my own devices, I am more likely to fill my cart with yards and yards of beautiful prints. Stocking up on solids, however—denims, khakis, chocolate brown, maybe a pink, some reds—is like stocking up on kitchen staples. Solids can be punched up with trims, appliqué, and other embellishments, and adding those are half the fun of sewing for kids.

I also like to have a lot of basic fabrics, such as striped knits, polka-dot percales, and ginghams, on hand. Sabine's second rule of thumb for purchasing fabric is to choose prints with small motifs only. The largest motif should be no larger than about 3 inches (7.5 cm) wide. Large prints are difficult to work into a garment and often distract from the garment's silhouette. If the scale is too large, the child will look upholstered instead of nicely dressed.

Buying fabric is just not the time to go cheap. Choose the nicest materials you can afford—you'll be making a better investment of your time and ideas. For everyday clothes, choose fabrics with a high natural fiber content (I use lots of cotton). These fabrics breathe, wash, and play the best. Choose fabrics intended for apparel. Quilter's and crafter's materials may not work well when made up as garments. Although synthetic-fiber velvet, taffeta, and organza are imitations of their traditional silk counterparts, they are a fine, more affordable, and easier-to-care-for choice for a child's fancy attire.

When you're sewing for kids, always make sure your fabrics and notions are free of hazardous materials and finishes. Heavy metals, such as lead, are still found in some fabric dyes and in screen-printed designs. Metal and plastic parts, such as zippers, buttons, cord toggles, lead crystals, and other notions can also be high in lead and harmful plastics. Small ones tend to chew and swallow things, but children are especially susceptible to the physical damage these substances can cause when they accumulate in the body. GOTS (Global Organic Textile Standard), Öko-Tex 100, Confidence in Textiles, and REACH are recognized manufac-

turing standards. Check the fabric bolt or ask your retailer whether the fabric meets these standards. In addition, you may want to take the production location and manufacturing practices of materials into consideration for environmental reasons. Unregulated and irresponsible textile production can be a major environmental polluter, so you may also want to consider the fabric manufacturer's practices as you make your fabric selection. In general, you can be assured of safety and standards if you choose goods that have been milled and dyed in the United States and the European Union.

MIX AND MATCH

A new sewing pattern is kind of like a new recipe. First, you try it out and see how you like it. Maybe you decide you'd like to add more of one spice and cut down on another. Once you have sewn a pattern you like, try mixing up the recipe and sew it again.

I spend hours cutting fabrics for different versions of the same favorite pattern. For example, I might gather a bunch of different jersey knits to make shirts. I cut all the parts of the shirt from one fabric and then cut them again in another fabric. It's a good way to use up my scraps, too. When I have the parts for four or five shirts stacked up, I can mix them all up: blue-striped bodice with red polka-dot sleeves fading into pink cuffs. I dig through trims and embellishments and add those to the piles, too. Then I put the piles into plastic bags, which become "kits" to sew as time allows.

tip!

The directions that accompany a garment pattern often suggest appropriate fabrics to ensure that the garment will fit and hang well. If you choose a different fabric, the result may be fine—but be aware that the fabric could change the look and fit of the garment.

Fabric Requirements

The yardage estimates provided for each project in this book as-
sume that you will make the entire garment in one fabric. On the
other hand, you can create a beautiful effect by combining several
fabrics in a single garment. If you decide to work with several different fabrics rather than one, you'll need to determine how much
yardage you'll need of each fabric. Cut out your tissue pattern
pieces. Mark an area that is the width of your folded fabric on a
table. Arrange the pattern pieces, indicating which fabric you'll
use for each. This process will help you estimate how much you
will need.

Fabric comes in a variety of widths. The narrower the fabric,
the more yards (or meters) you will need to make the garment. All
the yardage requirements for the projects in this book are calcu-
lated for 54-inch (1.4 m)-wide fabrics. If you are using a narrower
fabric, you will need to purchase more than the amount indicated
for the project; if you are working with a wider fabric, you will
need less fabric than indicated. Consult a fabric conversion chart
(easily found online) to calculate the yardage you'll need. Note
that the project yardage requirements do not include the extra
yardage needed for directional prints or matching repeats (the
interval at which a motif reappears along the fabric length).
Some fabrics may shrink, so you may need to buy extra yardage
to account for the shrinkage. As a general rule, purchase an extra
¼ yard (20 cm), just in case.

PHOTO
OF YOURSELF
NEXT TO A
STAR
$6.00
INCLUDING A FRAME
AND A FUN AUTOGRAPH

Sewing Room Must-Haves

Having the right sewing tools is like having the right shoes. You can dance better and hike farther if you're wearing the right shoes. Likewise, you'll make a better-fitting, better-looking garment in less time and with less effort if you are working with a machine (or machines) you love. You'll also want to keep on hand a few good tools specially designed for sewing—and a few that are not. Here's my list of sewing room must-haves:

Sewing Machines

A conventional sewing machine with a variety of zigzag stitches is essential and, in truth, all you really need to sew great clothes. A serger, or overlock machine, makes speedy work of many sewing tasks because it trims the seam allowance and sews and overcasts the seam all at once. A cover stitch machine—the machine that makes the double-stitched hems on commercially made T-shirts—is a luxury some just can't do without. But before you allow yourself to become seduced by machines that will thread your needle, embroider your jeans, do your taxes, and give you a pedicure, please keep this list of basic capabilities in mind. These are the features you really want in a machine:

- Adjustable speed control
- A strong motor for lots of piercing power
- Even and balanced stitches
- Automatic needle-down stop
- A good buttonhole function

Buy the best machine you can afford. The adage "You get what you pay for" applies more often than not. If your budget is limited, consider purchasing a good used machine from a dealer you trust and who has serviced the machine so it runs like new. I still occasionally use my mother's machine, which she purchased in the 1970s. It's a solid piece of fine Swiss manufacture that I will likely be able to give to my kids one day.

tip!

You might be tempted by that shade of forest green in your mother's sewing box, but never sew with old thread. It will break and fray. Save the cute wooden spool if you must, but put "forest green" on your shopping list and pick up a fresh spool on your next shopping trip.

• *This older machine doesn't have all the bells and whistles that new machines have, but for some things, like machine gathering, I think it actually works better.*

Small Gear

I seldom come away from a fabric store without acquiring some fantastic new gizmo to do that one little thingamajig. If I were to narrow down my collection to the tools I absolutely need for the projects in this book, however, this is what the list would look like:

Cutting Tools

Keep your cutting tools sharp—and out of reach of small children.
1. A good pair of tailor's shears (with offset handles)
2. Rotary cutters and cutting mat
3. Various seam rippers, thread snippers, and embroidery scissors

Pins, Needles, and Adhesives

Here are the essentials, plus a few that are just nice to have.
4. Straight pins (long, sharp, and thin, with glass heads, which won't melt under the iron), magnetized pin holder, and pincushion wristlet
5. Wonder Tape (a soluble basting tape, to affix trims and zippers before sewing) and safety pins
6. Needles: hand-sewing needles (sharps and quilter's) in several sizes; machine-sewing needles (for different types of fabrics)
7. Temporary aerosol adhesive spray (to affix appliqués before sewing)

Measuring and Marking Tools

These tools help you keep your work precise—when you want it that way.
8. Measuring tape
9. Marking tools (textile pencils, pens, disappearing ink pens, crayons, and chalks)
10. Seam gauge, hem gauge (for measuring or as a pressing template), and straight-edge (for drawing straight lines and rotary cutting)

Pressing and Organizing Gear

Always press as you sew! Pressing helps you stitch more accurately and ensures a crisp, professional finish.
11. Iron and ironing board (of course) and a finger presser (a small piece of wood with a beveled edge)
12. Utility apron with pockets (to keep small tools—and other necessities—close at hand)

Chapter 3

Measurements, Size, and Adjustments

Eager to start sewing? Stop right there! Put the shears down and step away from the fabric. That's it, nice and easy. Do not cut the fabric. The first step in making a great garment with an excellent fit is to measure the child. And measure. And measure again. Didn't you read the sign? "Measure thrice, cut once"? Always choose a pattern size based on your child's measurements and not his or her age or size in ready-to-wear.

On page 33 is a chart showing the basic measurements on which the patterns in this book are based. Each pattern size has been drafted with the appropriate wearing ease (the room needed for the garment to move comfortably with the wearer) and style ease (the proportions that make a garment close-fitting, average, or loose-fitting). After measuring your child, compare those measurements to the measurements on this chart to select the best-fitting pattern size as explained on page 34.

How to Measure

To measure your child, have your little one dressed in her underwear. If she's in diapers, measure her while she's wearing a diaper. Take the following measurements and record them on the table on page 32.

Height: With your barefoot child standing straight, measure from the top of the head to the floor.

Chest: Measure around the fullest part of the chest, under the arms and right under the shoulder blades.

Waist: Measure around the natural waistline, which is right above the navel.

Dropped waist: For a somewhat older child, who may not like the look of a high-waist trouser, measure below the navel, right at the top of the hip bone. Measure also the vertical measurement between the navel and the waistline. This measurement will indicate the amount of fabric that will need to be trimmed from the top edge of the trouser pieces.

Hip: Measure the fullest area around the hips and buttocks.

Shoulder width: Measure from the base of the neck to the edge of the arm.

Sleeve length: Have your child extend his arm straight out to the side and bend his elbow at a right angle straight up. Measure from the top of the shoulder over the bent elbow to the wrist bone.

Back neck-to-waist: Begin at the most prominent bone at the base of the neck and end at the natural waist, holding the measuring tape close to the body. Be sure to include those few extra centimeters or fractions of an inch over the round of the upper back.

Pants outseam: Measure from the natural waist over the round of the hips to the ankle bone.

Pants inseam: Measure from the inner ankle bone to the base of the crotch.

Crotch depth: While your child sits on a firm chair, feet flat on the floor (or flat on top of a stack of books), use a ruler to measure along the side of the body from the natural waistline to the seat of the chair.

Crotch line: Measure from the waistline at center front through the crotch to the waistline at center back.

Jacket length: Measure from the most prominent vertebra at the base of the neck to the hip bone (or to preferred jacket length).

Dress length: Measure from the most prominent vertebra at the base of the neck to below the knee (or to preferred dress length).

Minidress length: Measure from the most prominent vertebra at the base of the neck to above the knee.

Skirt length: Measure from the natural waist to below the knee (or to preferred skirt length).

Miniskirt length: Measure from the natural waist to above the knee.

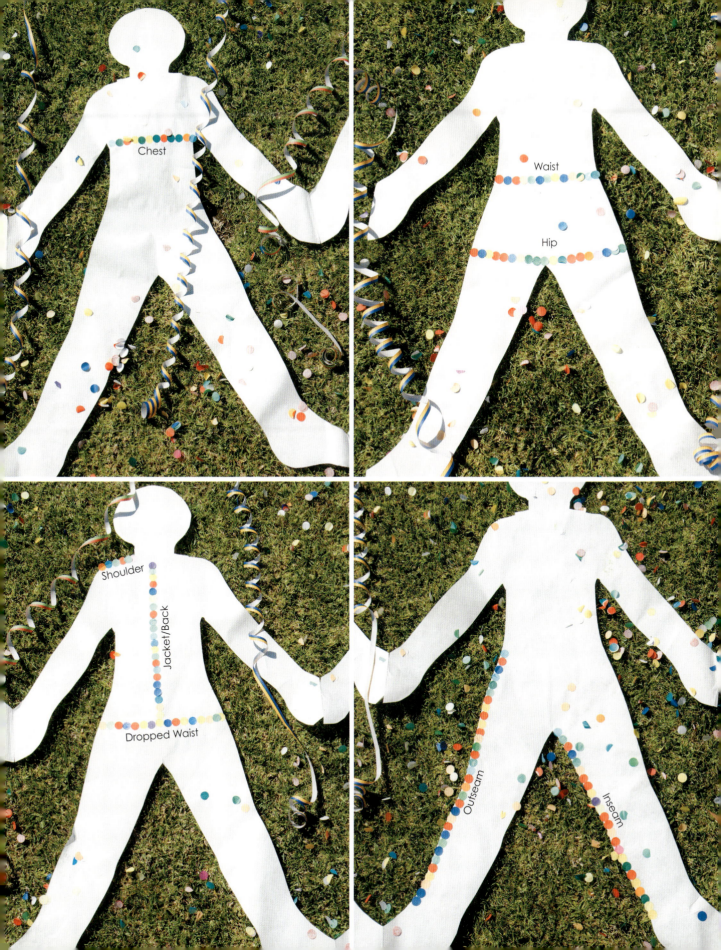

Child's Measurement Chart

	Child's Measurement	Pattern Measurement (total of all pieces that will be joined)	Amount of Difference (+ / −)
Height		————	————
Chest			
Waist			
Dropped Waist			
Hip			
Shoulder Width			
Sleeve Length			
Back Neck-to-Waist			
Pants Outseam			
Crotch Depth			
Crotch Line			
Jacket Length			
Minidress Length			
Dress Length			
Skirt Length			
Miniskirt Length			

Standard Body Measurements*

EU Size (height in cm)	Chest (cm)	Waist (cm)	Hips (cm)
86	55	52.3	56.3
92	56	52.5	56.5
98	57	53	58.0
104	58	53.5	59.5
110	59	54	61.0
116	60	55	62.5
122	62	56	65.5
128	64	58	68.5
134	66	59	71.5
140	68	60.5	74.5
146	72	62.5	78.5
152	76	64.5	82.5

*The patterns included in this book are based on the measurements in this chart.

How to Choose Size

To select a pattern size, compare the measurements you took of the child with the measurements in the Standard Body Measurements chart on page 33. Then find the pattern size that corresponds to the size in the chart. For a top, for example, you would compare your child's chest measurement with the chest measurements on the chart. Choose the size for which the chest is the same or, if there isn't an exact match, choose the next largest size. To select a pattern size for pants, compare the hip measurements. For a skirt, compare the waist measurements. Remember, the patterns include wearing and style ease, so the size of the tissue piece is not the size of the body—it's the size that is right for the style of the garment and will be comfortable to wear.

Most of the patterns in this book are loose fitting or can be adjusted with ties or elastic. If your child's waist is larger than the waist measurement that corresponds to the chest and hip measurement on the chart, however, it will be easier to alter the pattern at the waist than at the chest or hips—so don't choose a top or pants pattern size based on the garment's waist measurement.

SEWING STURDY HEMS

These patterns aren't drafted with hem allowances, so you'll need to add them (see page 36). Sewing basic hems is a simple matter of pressing and topstitching. Use these methods for all the projects, unless otherwise indicated.

For garments made of knit fabric, fold under the given hem allowance and press. Then pin or baste the hem. Topstitch with a stretch or cover stitch, sewing close to the raw edge of the hem allowance.

For garments made of woven fabrics, make a double-folded hem. Fold the hem allowance under and press. Then, fold the raw edge of the allowance in to meet the crease you just made. Press the hem again and pin or baste. Topstitch with a straight stitch, close to the inner fold.

"Because the forms and silhouettes of fashion change from season to season, few other industries are subject to the whims of trend as is the apparel industry. Nonetheless, the basics of pattern construction remain the same. The goal of pattern making is an optimal fit, regard less of current trends. Children's clothing construction requires different considerations from adult clothing. Im portant aspects for chil dren are a high degree of comfort, generous freedom of movement for play, functionality, independence in dress ing and undressing, as well as a look that is suitable and special for a child in the form of the garment."
—Anja Müssig

About the Patterns

Couture drafter Anja Müssig hand-drafted the patterns you'll find in the enclosed pattern envelope. Anja is the owner of the pattern company Schnittreif and is a marvelous clothing designer in her own right, with an impressive list of European fashion houses on her resume. Anja helps us make the best sewing patterns possible. She is responsible for the excellent fit and form of these designs: the tiny tapers adding flare here, subtracting volume there, creating negative space here, and comfort there—all are a part of the art of the pattern drafter. She works with pencil and ruler, and drafts every bit by hand, from inception to finished pattern, until, as she says, "the patterns are, in the truest sense, *schnittreif* (scissors ready)."

The enclosed patterns for the projects are made in the European tradition. They have somewhat different markings than American sewing patterns. Instead of notches, for example, there are short lines printed across the seamline to indicate where two pieces should align. Most important, the patterns do not include seam allowances. Patterns without seam allowances, like these, are sometimes called slopers. (The term *sloper* also refers to a basic pattern for a garment, which provides the basis for other garment sizes or styles.) I like the flexibility of patterns without seam allowances. Because each piece represents the actual garment section, I can more easily visualize the finished garment and its fit and length. Also, depending on the type of seam I'm planning to use, I have the option to change the width of the seam allowance— to use less fabric for serger construction, for example, or to use a full 1-inch (2.5 cm) seam allowance, as in couture sewing (as my mother taught me). A sloper allows you to sew according to your preference—but you must remember to add the allowances as you cut out the garment pieces!

You'll need to add hem allowances as you cut, too. How much you add depends on how you plan to finish the bottom edge. If I'm adding a ruffle, for example, I use a ⅜-inch (1 cm) allowance. If not, I use a ¾-inch (2 cm) allowance, so I can turn the edge under twice for a narrow hem. If you're not sure how long the garment should be, add a deeper allowance and check the length later, while fitting the garment.

Pattern Tracing and Seam Allowances

All of our patterns are multisized. You can either cut out the size you need or, better yet, trace a copy of the size so you can make another size of the garment from the original pattern later.

You can trace the pattern onto several types of materials: the pattern tracing materials found in fabric stores, poly fiber, landscaper's cloth, poster paper, tissue paper, and clear plastic sheeting. You can also transfer the pattern to muslin with dressmaker's carbon and a tracing wheel.

Before tracing, press the pattern sheets with a warm, dry iron to remove the creases. Locate the line style that indicates the size you wish to sew (you'll find a key to the line styles and equivalent sizes on each pattern sheet). Be sure to transfer the grain line and the marks. Label each pattern piece with the identifying number printed on the original pattern.

After tracing the pattern outline, draw the seam allowance around it, working with a seam gauge or transparent grid ruler as a guide. You can also use your rotary cutter, fitted with an adjustable guide, to cut on the allowance. Some people like to "sew" the drawn allowance on the tracing with an unthreaded sewing machine; the stitching perforates the tissue so you can tear off the excess easily. Others prefer to add the seam allowance when they cut out the garment instead. They then draw the seamline onto the fabric for reference during construction. Whichever method you choose, just be sure to add the seam allowance accurately so that your pieces will fit together correctly when you sew.

Adjusting the Pattern

I suggest that you take more measurements than the ones on the standard measurements chart, because the information will be useful if you want to make alterations before you cut the fabric—to adjust the length of a top, skirt, pants, or sleeve, for example. You can measure the length of a pattern piece—say, a pant-leg outseam or the center back of a jacket—and compare the measurement to your child's measurement for that same area. If there is a difference (especially if the pattern is short), you will want to adjust the pattern before you cut the fabric. If the pattern is fairly straight, you can add or subtract at the hem. If the pattern flares or tapers, adjust it in the middle of the flared area, either by folding out the excess or by cutting the pattern horizontally, separating the two pieces, and adding length between them (by taping on another piece of tissue to fill the gap). Then, simply redraw the flared outline over your fold or patch.

If your child's crotch line is longer than the pattern's, you should add pattern length above the waist. It can be tricky to figure out exactly how much to add, or where to add it, however. The difference might be due to a large tummy or derriere or to a long torso. The best approach is to add a bit more length than you think you need and refine the fit later when the child tries on the garment during construction.

Perhaps the child's waist is large relative to the standard chest or hip measurement for the garment size. If so, find the difference by subtracting the standard waist size from your child's waist measurement. Then divide the difference by four and add the result to each piece at the side seam, tapering the new width into the existing seamline at the lower hip or chest level. This method works if the amount to be added is not more than 1 or 2 inches (2.5 or 5 cm) and if the child is fairly straight through the torso. If the child has a bit of a tummy, however, you'll probably need to add more width to the front. (See page 39 for some ideas on how to make this adjustment.)

SIMPLE PLUS-SIZE ALTERATIONS

Sewing plus-sized clothes is a great alternative for the parent and child who walk out of the shopping mall again and again in disappointment, maybe even tears, because there is nothing fun and fashionable that fits. A stocky stature has different proportions from an average build, so just using a larger pattern size may not work—the "plus" proportions are usually larger in some areas than in others. Instead, start with the closest pattern size. Choose the size as you would for a standard body (see page 33) and make a muslin sample of the garment. You'll bring a smile to your child's face, after all. Not all patterns can be easily altered for all bodies, but here are some things to try.

Saggy Seat

One problem plus-sized kids might have with trousers is that the seat of the pants sags. One way to remedy this problem is to cut the trousers so the top edge rests at the hip bone, rather than at the natural waist. Make a muslin sample with the waist in the usual place, adding girth at the side seams and center front to fit the child comfortably. Have the child put on the muslin and then draw a dropped waistline at her high hip.

Large Waist and Hips

If your child is large at the waist and hips, make a muslin sample of a skirt pattern, adding girth at the side seams and center front. Fit the muslin until it hangs well.

Heavy Thighs

If the child has heavy thighs, adding girth through the waist and hip area may not be enough for a good fit. Slash the pattern vertically from the waist to the knees (or to the hem) and spread the pieces to add the necessary amount of width. Then redraw the outseam (and inseam) with nicely tapered lines. Be careful, or you're likely to change the grain line of the pattern when you do this—experiment in muslin to make sure you like the results. If necessary, consult a good fitting book or search for more detailed information online.

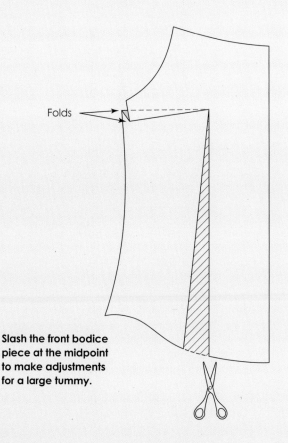

Folds

Slash the front bodice piece at the midpoint to make adjustments for a large tummy.

Big Tummy

To adjust shirts, jackets, and tops to fit over large tummies and hips, slash the front pattern vertically from the hem to the chest or shoulders. As shown in the drawing above, draw a line parallel to the center front, approximately halfway across the traced front pattern piece. Cut on this line, stopping at a level just below the armhole.

Then spread the sections apart at the hemline. Pivot the side section out, spreading it to create a gap at the hemline equal to one-half the amount you wish to add. The pattern tissue will lift to form a dart from under the armhole to the top of the slash; fold this dart down against the tissue. At the bottom of the side seam, add the length lost by the dart, tapering this amount into the original hemline toward the center (tape on more tissue if you need to). If your child has round upper hips, you may want to make the same alteration in the back, spreading the front and back pieces each by one-quarter the total amount to be added.

Chapter 4

Fitting, Laying Out, and Cutting

Fitting is part of sewing. If you take time to fit, you'll be sure to make a comfortable garment that flatters your child. You may fit directly on your child, or, if you prefer to work with a model that has infinite patience, on a kinderquin—a dummy you can easily make that duplicates the child's form (see page 43).

Fitting

There are three basic ways to fit—by tissue fitting, making a muslin, and fitting during construction—and good reasons for each. In each method, you refine the fit by adjusting the pinned or basted seams and hemlines. Mark new seamlines with pencil or chalk. If you are working with a tissue or muslin sample, take the sample apart and transfer the new lines to the tissue pattern. If you don't have enough seam allowance to make a needed adjustment, patch on more tissue or sample fabric with pins or tape. When fitting during construction, you may need to redo the seams or add a creative seam in order to adjust the fit.

Tissue Fitting

If you add generous seam allowance to your traced pattern before cutting it out, you can pin it together and have your child try it on before you cut your fabric. Hold the tissue pieces together with small sticky notes, and there'll be no complaints of pin pricks. If you trace onto a fabric-like material, you may be able to baste the pattern together to check the fit.

Making a Muslin

The most accurate fitting method is creating a muslin sample—either from muslin or any other inexpensive cloth. The sample is only for fitting, so just cut the principal pieces (no facings, collars, or pockets), baste them together, and have the child try on the sample. If you are reasonably sure the fit will be a success, you could choose to make the sample in a fabric you like and finish it to make a wearable garment.

Fitting during Construction

After sewing together each principal section of the garment (no facings, collars, or pockets), and before going on to the next step, have the child try on the garment. If you've had a good muslin fitting, you may not need to fit during the construction process, but different fabrics may work up a bit differently, so it's always a good idea to double-check the fit.

Making a Kinderquin Dress Form

The kinderquin is a custom dress form of your child. Kinderquin is my term—a combination of *kinder*, the German word for child, and mannequin. Instead of paying $100 or more for a standard dressmaker's form, for a fraction of that, you can make a form that exactly replicates your child's shape in about an hour. Not only is this a fun little project, but you'll also have a useful tool to help you while you're fitting and designing your child's garment.

Make the kinderquin from duct tape and a T-shirt and leggings or tights that fit your child snugly—and that you don't mind sacrificing to the "good fit" cause. You'll also need a pair of bandage scissors (designed to cut away cloth bandages without poking the wearer and sold at pharmacies). You can work with standard shears instead, but be sure to place your hand between the scissors and the child's body so you don't inadvertently hurt your little one as you cut.

To begin, dress the child in the T-shirt and leggings or tights. Pull the T-shirt taut over the leggings or tuck the hem into the waistband—you don't want the duct tape to make contact with any skin. Ouch!

Wrapping

Cut strips of duct tape in various lengths, ranging from approximately 6 to 18 inches (15.2 to 45.7 cm). Smooth the T-shirt against the child's skin so it lies flat without bunching anywhere. Secure the shirt to the leggings with a few strips of duct tape.

Adhere strips of duct tape to the T-shirt, fitting the tape snugly (but comfortably) around the child's stomach and chest. Apply duct tape to just the shoulder or all the way down the sleeve. Leave

• *The first step to making a dress form: have your child don an old T-shirt and leggings or tights.*

• *Secure the T-shirt tautly with duct tape strips of varying lengths.*

• *Wrap the entire kinderquin with two layers of tape.*

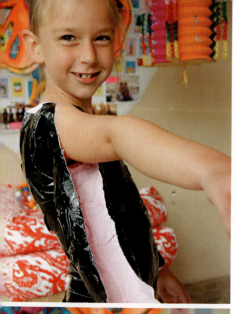

• Cut the kinderquin up one side.

• Fill the kinderquin with poly fiberfill and/or fabric scraps until the form is firm.

• Hang the kinderquin from the hanger hook to make it easier to fit the garment.

a generous area around the neckline free of tape. Now tape around the buttocks and thighs, extending the wrapping to about mid-thigh. Try to wrap two layers of duct tape over the entire kinderquin.

Cutting Away

Cut through the duct tape and garments along one side of the child's body, working from the thigh to the chest—and along the length of the arm if that's taped, too. If necessary, cut just enough at the other wrist for the child to pull her hand through. Remove the duct-tape shell from the child (cutting further as needed). Then cover the cut edges with duct tape to join them together again.

Trim the bottoms of the leggings or tuck them into the kinderquin thighs. Tape the thigh and arm or wrist openings to close them. From the neck opening, insert a few small stones into the thighs to weight the form. If the stones are balanced evenly, the kinderquin will stand on its own.

Filling

Fill the kinderquin with poly fiberfill and/or fabric scraps. If you have included the arms, do not stuff them firmly. They should remain flexible so you can dress and undress the kinderquin. Before filling the shoulders, insert a sturdy clothes hanger into the neck. (A hanger with curved shoulders works best.) Continue filling until the body is firm. Close the neck and hanger opening with more duct tape. Form a neck with the tape as best you can.

You now have a custom-made dress form. It is not especially pretty, but it is much less fidgety than its subject, stays home from school, and is permitted to stay up way past bedtime for fitting sessions. You can even stick pins into it! The small stones you inserted in the bottom will help the kinderquin stand, but it's easier and more practical to hang it while you work.

Laying Out and Cutting

Now that you have found the perfect fit, you're ready to lay out and cut the garment pattern pieces. I'm a big advocate of washing fabric before cutting. Washing removes the chemical finishes, softens the fabric, and preshrinks (to avoid surprises later). You also want to be sure that your fabric isn't off grain (when the crosswise threads are not perpendicular to the selvages, the woven edges of the fabric). If it is, your finished garment won't hang nicely. To ensure the grain is straight, firmly pull the fabric diagonally from end to end. A careful pressing may also help, as will drying the fabric on a clothesline with the opposite selvages pinned together. Always press fabric after washing to remove wrinkles; if it's flimsy, a light spray of starch may make it easier to handle.

When you're ready to cut your garment, spread the fabric flat on a worktable. If the pattern pieces are large and asymmetrical, you will cut them from a single layer. Very often patterns can be cut with the fabric folded in half. Most often, it's more economical to fold the fabric lengthwise, bringing the two selvages together at one edge. Folding the fabric so that both selvages meet in the middle gives you two folds in a short length, which is sometimes a good option for children's clothes when the pieces are not large. Another economical way to cut is to fold one edge over just enough to cut some pieces from a double layer and the other pieces from the single layer.

The directions for each project in this book indicate how many of each pattern piece you need to cut. Each pattern piece is marked with a grain line to indicate how it should be aligned on the straight grain of the fabric. When you lay out the pattern on your fabric, place this grain line parallel to the selvage. If the pattern piece indicates the piece should be cut on the fold, place the fold line on the fold of your fabric. Secure the pieces with pins or weights.

There are no cutting layouts for these projects—we hope you'll use more than one fabric for each garment—so just be sure to arrange all the pieces before cutting any of them. If you did not add seam allowances to your patterns, be sure to leave space between the pieces so you can add the allowances now. Transfer match marks, darts, and similar information from the pattern to each fabric piece with dressmaker's carbon.

tips!

• On knit fabrics, the lengthwise grain lies along one vertical line of knit stitches. Some knits do not have true selvages, so look closely to find the grain, which may not be parallel to the edge.

• After you've cut the pieces, make a masking tape label with the piece number or name and affix it to the wrong side of the fabric—especially important if there are several pieces that could easily be confused.

Chapter 5

Sewing and Embellishing

When constructing a garment, the devil is in the details. In embellishing the garment, the angel is in the details. With the right techniques and some care, handmade clothes can look just as professional as manufactured garments, but with a charm all their own. The patterns and instructions in this book show you how to put the pieces of each garment together—but when adding embellishment, let your creative mind take control. I'll share some construction basics. I'll also share some of my favorite embellishment techniques, but the "what" you use, "how" you use it, and the "where," "when," and "why" are up to you. These patterns are road maps; you determine the journey.

Three Keys to Success

Just about anyone can sew the projects in this book. If I can, you can. The construction techniques require only basic sewing knowledge and a little experience. There are three keys to great sewing. Follow these simple steps, and each of your finished garments will be a great success.

Check the Machine Settings

Test before you sew! You may have to adjust the thread tension in order to sew pucker-free seams on different fabrics. Depending on the fabrics and number of layers you're working with, you may have to adjust the foot pressure so the fabric feeds smoothly through the machine.

Finish before You're Done

Finishing is the practice of securing the cut edge of the fabric so it won't ravel. One method of finishing is to serge or zigzag the edges of all your fabric pieces before you sew them together. Another method is to overcast both seam allowances together after you've sewn the seam. This second method is usually preferable for children's clothing because it offers another line of defense against tension during wear, which might split the seam later. If, however, the sewing instructions call for the seam allowances to be pressed open and topstitched on each side of the seam, finish these fabric edges ahead of time.

Pressing Matters

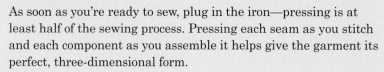

As soon as you're ready to sew, plug in the iron—pressing is at least half of the sewing process. Pressing each seam as you stitch and each component as you assemble it helps give the garment its perfect, three-dimensional form.

Two Essential Techniques

Two techniques I use often are gathering (for skirts, ruffles, and sleeve caps) and French seams (for a great, classic finish without a serger or zigzag stitch).

Gathering

Gathering is easy to do. Just sew two lines of basting along the fabric edge that you wish to gather and then pull the bobbin threads. To achieve even gathers, use the shortest basting stitch that will neatly distribute the gathers in the type of fabric you are using. Heavy fabrics and tightly woven fabrics with a high thread count require a long basting stitch; lightweight, loosely woven fabrics (such as voile and batiste, for example) are best gathered with a shorter stitch. Here are a few tips that will help make the process of gathering easier to control.

- Use a bobbin filled with heavy-duty thread.
- Sew with the fabric right-side up. For easier handling, gather long edges in sections about 2 feet (60 cm) long.
- Pull both bobbin threads gently to gather the fabric. As shown at right, insert a pin perpendicular to the end of the gathering. Then wrap the bobbin threads in a figure eight around the pin to temporarily secure the fullness.
- Pin the gathered piece at intervals to the piece you are sewing it to. If you need to loosen or tighten the gathers, unwrap the figure-eight wrapping and adjust the bobbin threads.

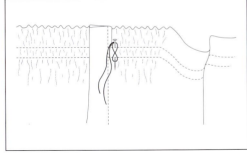

If the edge I'm gathering is very long, rather than basting and then pulling bobbin threads, I adjust the machine to gather the fabric for me. A special ruffling presser foot is available for most sewing machines. If you have an older machine that doesn't automatically adjust the thread tension, as I do, just increase the tension of the upper thread; then when you sew, the fabric "gathers" as it passes under the presser foot. Often I secure the gathered stitching line with a line of zigzag stitching. Other times, as shown at lower right, I sew a piece of single-fold bias tape over the gathering stitches on the wrong side of the fabric. There is quite a bit of tension on the gathering threads, so if you don't secure the gathers, the threads might break, causing the gathered area to come apart.

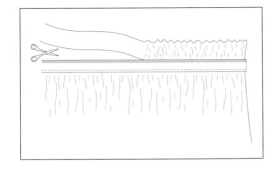

French Seams

A French seam is actually made up of two seams. The fabric is sewn, folded to enclose the raw edges, and sewn again. This seam makes a very neat finish and is a good choice for sheer fabrics and for unlined jackets—anywhere you don't wish to catch a glimpse of overcasting stitches or frayed edges. Here are the four basic steps.

1 Pin the pieces to be joined with their wrong sides together. Sew ⅜ inch (1 cm) from the edge using a straight stitch.

2 Trim the seam allowances to about ⅛ inch (3 mm).

3 Open the fabric layers and press the seam allowances to one side. Now, bring the right sides together and fold the fabric along the seam. Press along the seam.

4 Sew ¼ inch (6 mm) from the fold.

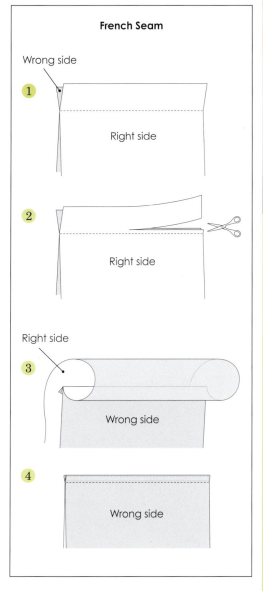

French Seam

1 — Wrong side / Right side

2 — Right side

3 — Right side / Wrong side

4 — Wrong side

ESSENTIAL STITCHES

Here is a list of the stitches I find most useful along with some tips.

• **Straight stitch.** The basic stitch for seams and topstitching on woven fabrics

• **Zigzag stitch.** For seams on knits or finishing edges on any fabric if you don't have a serger

• **Three-step zigzag stitch.** A strong zigzag that keeps the fabric flat inside the stitching; good for topstitching knits or applying elastic for gathering

• **Blanket stitch.** A zigzag variation that works well for finishing edges or attaching fabric or trim when you just want to catch the edge

• **Four-thread overedge stitch.** The basic serger stitch; good for construction or edge finishing

• **Three-thread overedge stitch.** Similar to the four-thread overedge stitch, but not as strong and best for finishing edges

• **Three-thread rolled hem.** A very tightly overcast, fine hem; use contrasting thread for extra definition

• **Rolled hem on a conventional machine.** Neat, narrow, and more discreet than a serger rolled hem; sewn with a straight stitch; requires special presser foot

Working with Knits

Sewing knit fabrics may feel a bit different from sewing woven fabric, but there's nothing to fear. In fact, because most seams on a knit garment require no topstitching, knit sewing projects are usually very quick to make. You also don't need to be as exact when cutting knits as when cutting wovens, because the give in the knit fabric allows you to stretch a piece that doesn't quite match its mate as you sew. To prevent damage to knits, always sew them with a ballpoint needle.

The preferred machine for sewing knits is a serger, which creates a seam with stretch while finishing the edge at the same time. You can also sew knits with a standard sewing machine, of course, if you keep a few things in mind. Whether you use a serger or a conventional machine, be sure to test the stitches on a scrap of your fabric and adjust the settings and presser foot pressure as needed.

Knit fabrics stretch, so machine-sew with thread that has some give, such as polyester or nylon; cotton thread is likely to break as the knit fabric stretches. I also recommend sewing with a very narrow simple or three-step zigzag stitch instead of a straight stitch because these stitches will give with the fabric. (For a loose-fitting knit garment, like the Imke shirt on page 61, a straight stitch will work fine if you use a polyester sewing thread.) After you sew each seam, finish it with a mock overcast or blanket stitch.

If you do not have much experience sewing knits, stick with tightly knit varieties that are easy to work with—sturdy cotton interlock or single jersey, perhaps with a bit of Spandex, or a thermal fleece. If you use single jersey, keep in mind that the cut edges will roll, so be sure to keep that steam iron warm and ready to press them flat before stitching.

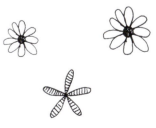

Creative Embellishment

For me, the sewing process begins with pencil and paper. I make a rough sketch of the garment, drawing in the lines for seams. The drawing helps me think through the project and explore design options—a helpful step, especially if some design choices will affect the construction sequence or methods. So before you begin your project, get comfortable and read through the directions carefully. Have paper and pencil nearby to make notes as you read. Roughly sketch out the design and staple scraps of the fabric to your sketch. Look at the photos in this book for ideas. Think about where you would like to add embellishments and add them to your sketch.

Embellishments are a way to add surprise to a garment—and makes getting dressed a treasure hunt for my daughter. I love hearing her excited voice when she notices a little something in the lining or on the underskirt, "Mom! Look! It's so cute!" I include ribbons, braids, rickrack, and other trims, machine embroidery, iron-on transfers, appliqué, ruffles, and ruching. I use embellishments alone and in combination. I have fun with them, and you should do the same. Most of the time, an embellishment needs to be incorporated as you assemble the garment, but serendipity works, too—I'm all for covering booboos with embellishments. When you're ready to start sewing, have several trims at the ready. You'll change your mind as you go and the one trim you thought didn't even match just may be the one that pulls the entire design together.

tip!

Make sure embellishments won't pose a danger to small children who chew and swallow dangling things. I often add small loops to designs for my seven-year-old, who likes to hang key chains and other knickknacks to personalize her outfit. But I wouldn't add this kind of embellishment to the garments of very young children or their older siblings.

Ribbons and Trims

I love pretty trims. I probably spend more on trims than on fabrics! Adding row upon row of carefully mixed trims is an easy detail that will immediately set your handmade item apart from any item at the best boutique. My German sewing friends use the term *Tüddeltante* to describe those of us who sit on the floor ankle deep in ribbons, trims, and embellishments, adding more and more stuff (*Tüddelei*) to the garment.

Need romance? French taffeta ombré. Have a special occasion? Velvet ribbon. Want vintage style or a way to maneuver curves? Rickrack. Need a casual look? Gingham ribbon. Need to add definition to a hem? Bias tape. Looking for big fun? Ball fringe.

What is my very favorite embellishment in the arsenal? Bright-patterned ribbons. I love the ribbons with intricately woven designs. My eye is drawn immediately to the little characters and pretty forms woven into them. Even my son's friends, as they parade through my house, clip off bits of a certain hedgehog woven tape to wear as bracelets.

One trim is seldom enough, in my opinion. Anywhere you add a ruffle, there is room to put a line of rickrack in the seam too. A line of ribbon along the lower edge will really make a ruffle stand out. If you are going to the trouble to add ruching (see page 76), it doesn't take any more effort to sew a line of tiny rickrack down its center. A handful of brightly colored ribbons dangling from a skirt can cast a magic spell, causing the wearer to dance and spin herself silly. A few on the tip of a pointed hood add a touch of whimsy.

Polyester ribbons are best for lacing and cinching because they are strong and slide easily through loops. Printed ribbons can fade with washing, but polyester woven tapes are colorfast, so there is very little risk of bleeding. Silk trims and tapes have many of the properties of polyester, but offer a special feel and sheen. Quality trims are tightly woven and have no loose threads on the wrong side. Loosely woven tapes are likely to fray.

tip!

Fold a bit of patterned ribbon into a loop. Add it to the side seam of a shirt or slip it under the edge of a patch pocket. It will look like one of the "signature" clothing tags some designers use.

When incorporating trims and ribbons into your garment, keep in mind that most will not follow a curve. They tend to work only in straight lines—up the center of a sleeve, for example, or around a pant cuff. If you want trim to travel in curves and swirls, choose bias tape, rickrack, braids, ruches, or elasticized trims. Or gather one edge of the ribbon, and it will curve nicely.

Think through the trim application before you begin to sew. If you wish to add trim across only one section of a garment—for example, the back panel of a jacket—apply it before sewing that section to another section; this way, the ends of the trim will be concealed in the seam. If the trim does not end at joining seams, either tuck under the end of the trim or finish it with very small zigzag stitches to prevent raveling. If a trim extends all around a garment—at the hem, for example—add it as a last step; to finish, overlap the ends, turning under the

end on top. Before stitching, I adhere trims with Wonder Tape, but a few pins will do the trick.

Machine Embroidery

Machine-embroidered designs provide a great way to express the mood and theme of a garment. Add a skull-and-crossbones motif to a conservative plaid fabric, and you've got punk style. Embroider roses on camouflage, and the finished effect is pure romance. Machine embroidery allows me to incorporate the fun and whimsy of very talented graphic artists into my own designs. If your machine is not equipped to embroider, some online retailers provide stitched-out designs on felt or another fabric backing. You can sew these embroidery "patches" directly onto your fabric.

Plan carefully if you wish to embroider directly on the garment. It's best to

embroider the fabric before cutting. Make a chalk outline of the paper pattern piece on the fabric, hoop the fabric, and then embroider. Position the paper pattern over the embroidered motif and then cut out the pattern piece. Alternatively, you may want to add embroidery to an already constructed garment. Lay the hoop over the garment, draw the hoop outline with chalk, remove the hoop, and then hold up the garment to make sure the placement is where you want it. If it is, reposition the hoop and stitch. You could also embroider the motif on a separate piece of matching fabric, cut it out, and sew it to the garment as an appliqué. If you choose this method, leave a bit of extra fabric outside the stitched lines; then clip along the edges to allow the fabric to fray and add texture.

Instructions for each embroidery design suggest thread colors, but use whatever colors you wish. Also, look for opportunities while embroidering to include other materials—for example, bits of dangling ribbon or yarn to make hair or bird's legs. The embroidery design instructions will tell you when to add these extra elements. Keep a stack of embroidered patches nearby—not only are they a lot of fun, they also make great Band-Aids for an ugly tear.

Iron-on Transfers

Iron-on transfers are bits of instant gratification: just a few seconds under the iron, and there you have it! Much like machine embroidery, transfers offer an excellent way to add graphic design elements to an outfit to reinforce the style or theme. They look very professional and, best of all, are very easy to apply. The adhering webs and materials of iron-on transfers have improved quite a bit since I was a kid, and today's transfers will last for many wash-

ings. Iron-on transfers often have a flocked or vinyl surface that introduces a new texture to the garment.

I believe that, for children's clothing, "more is more," and combining iron-on transfers with embroidery, ribbon, appliqué, and all other manner of embellishment is just the thing to do. I like to experiment with placement—adding transfers in unexpected places, like sleeves. I occasionally overlap transfers and incorporate them in traditional machine appliqué (see page 71). Plus, with proper supervision, the selection, placement, and adhering of transfers is something an older child can do himself to personalize his outfit.

Iron-on transfers work best when the adhering web fuses with the fibers of the fabric. So, they don't last long on some synthetic materials, such as waterproof nylon or acetate satin. If you apply transfers to denim, jersey, or percale, however, you can

expect your child to outgrow the garment before the transfer flakes or peels.

For most iron-on transfers, it is important to wait for the transfer to cool for several seconds before removing the backing. Follow the manufacturer's instructions for the transfer you're using. I sometimes ask the vendor for a small scrap of the iron-on medium to test on my fabric if I've never used it before. Many online, home-based suppliers will go the extra mile to help you understand their products.

You'll find lots of other ideas and embellishment techniques in the projects throughout this book. Don't be afraid to get creative, mix and match, experiment, and explore to make the truly one-of-a-kind clothes that your kids (and you!) will love.

Sewing the Projects

The projects in this book feature a variety of colorful designs and garment types, including shirts, jackets, skirts, pants, and leggings. Each project will teach you a new technique, which you may then apply to other projects if you are inspired. Each project also presents a sidebar that focuses on a particular skill or technique that you'll apply to that project. Each also offers a design variation, so you can explore the sewing skills at your own pace and comfort level. You'll find the multisized patterns in the pattern envelope attached to the book's front cover.

I've tried to give you a quick introduction to each garment and from time to time will present a few hints that you should keep in mind—but really, the best way to learn is by doing!

You can make the projects in the order they are presented here—from "Simple to Sew" to "Masterpiece," or you can refer to the button-dot code (expained below and found on the opening page of each project) and choose the projects that best suit you as you continue to develop your skills:

⊕ Simple to Sew

This project has few pattern pieces, a limited number of easy techniques, and few steps.

⊕ ⊕ Intermediate

This project has a more complex design and requires some additional skills, such as gathering, inserting a zipper, piecing, and bagging a lining, for example.

⊕ ⊕ ⊕ Masterpiece

This project has many design details and numerous steps, including, for example, lining garments, creating internal casings for elastic, and making and attaching button loops.

Have fun and enjoy your sewing adventures!

Projects

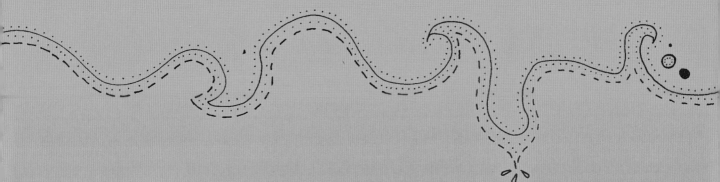

Imke Shirt

Here is an everyday, everywhere shirt for both boys and girls. This Imke design is a simple shirt with many different design options. It's also a good project for practicing the flat method of construction, in which the sleeves are set in before the side seams are closed and the side and sleeve seams are sewn in one pass.

There are two bodice versions and several different sleeve options, so you can tailor it for each gender and each child. One bodice style is straight—a good choice for boys or girls who want a more traditional look. The tapered bodice was designed specifically for girls. The short sleeve can be worn alone or as a layered cap over any of the long sleeves. To create a T-shirt look, use the neckband option. To make a custom-crafted hoody, add the hood—either rounded for a sporty style or pointed for a winsome charm.

Recommended Fabrics:

- knit fabrics only, with 20% to 25% stretch across the grain (page 75)
- 100% cotton or 98% cotton/2% Spandex-blend jersey
- interlock knits
- Polar fleece
- knit velour
- knit panné velvet

Notions

- polyester or nylon sewing thread

Pattern Piece Cutting List: Pattern Sheet 1

- (1/2 for boys, 5/6 for girls) Bodice front: Cut one on the fold. If using side panels, separate 5/6 along marked line and cut only the center section.

- (1/2 for boys, 5/6 for girls) Bodice back: Cut one on the fold. If using side panels, separate 5/6 along marked line and cut only the center section.

- (5/6) Side panels (optional): Separate the side panel from the bodice front/back and cut four.

- (3 straight sleeve; or 7 flared sleeve for girls) Sleeves: Cut two on fold.

- (8) Gathered sleeve caps: Cut two on the fold.

- (4) Hood piece (optional): Cut two or, for a lined hood, cut four.

- Neckband, if not adding a hood: Cut one strip of fabric on the cross grain 2" (5 cm) wide and slightly longer than the neck seamline.

Sewing Imke

Before cutting your fabric, make a few design decisions: First, decide if you want to include the side panels or leave the front and back plain. Also decide whether you would prefer a hood (lined or unlined) or a neckband. Finally, decide what type of sleeves you want: short, long, layered, straight, or flared.

Sketch your design (page 52), select the appropriate pattern pieces for your garment, and trace them if desired (see page 36). Lay the pieces on the prewashed, pressed fabric and cut them (page 45). Pay attention to the grain line of the pattern piece. It should be parallel to the ribs of the fabric. Then transfer all the marks from the pattern to the fabric. The side panels look somewhat similar in both directions, so mark the front and back with a sticky note or a piece of masking tape.

note: *Sew all the seams with the fabric right sides together unless otherwise indicated. For construction seams, use a four-thread overlock stitch on a serger or a stretch stitch on a conventional machine. For topstitching, use a stretch stitch, such as a three-step zigzag or a three-thread cover-stitch.*

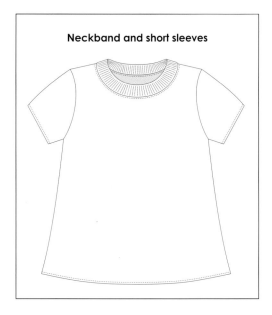

Neckband and short sleeves

Size Chart

Size	18 mos.–2T 86/92		3T–4T 98/104		5T–6 110/116		7–8 122/128		9–10 134/140		11–12 146/152	
	US	EURO	US	EURO	US	EURO	US	EURO	US	EURO	US	EURO
Chest Circumference	25"	64 cm	26"	66 cm	26¾"	68 cm	28⅜"	72 cm	30"	76 cm	33"	84 cm
Shoulder Width	2⅜"	6 cm	2⅜"	6 cm	2½"	6.5 cm	2⅞"	7 cm	3⅛"	8 cm	3⅜"	8.5 cm
Sleeve Length	11½"	29 cm	13"	33 cm	14½"	37 cm	16½"	42 cm	18½"	47 cm	20¼"	51.5 cm
Front Bodice Length	14¼"	37 cm	15¾"	40 cm	17¼"	44 cm	18⅞"	48 cm	20½"	52 cm	22⅞"	58.5 cm

Pointed hood with pieced bodice and sleeves

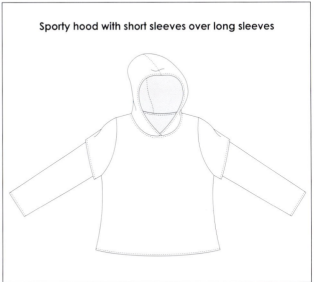

Sporty hood with short sleeves over long sleeves

Fabric Requirements Table

Size	Fabric Width	18 mos.–2T 86/92		3T–4T 98/104		5T–6 110/116		7–8 122/128		9–10 134/140		11–12 146/152	
		US	EURO	US	EURO	US	EURO	US	EURO	US	EURO	US	EURO
Without Hood	54" (140 cm)	⅝ yd	45 cm	⅝ yd	50 cm	⅝ yd	55 cm	1⅛ yd	100 cm	1¼ yd	110 cm	1¼ yd	120 cm
With Hood	54" (140 cm)	¾ yd	75 cm	⅞ yd	81 cm	1 yd	87 cm	1⅜ yd	134 cm	1½ yd	145 cm	1⅞ yd	156 cm

Amount required to make the entire garment in one fabric.

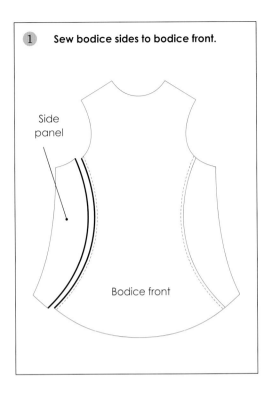

① Sew bodice sides to bodice front.

Side panel

Bodice front

Sew the Bodice

1 If you are not using the side panels, go to step 3. If you are using the side panels, sew them to the bodice front.

2 Sew the side panels to the bodice back.

3 Sew the bodice front to the bodice back at one shoulder seam. If your fabric is lightweight or fragile, reinforce the seam with seam tape, narrow ribbon, or clear elastic. Now, depending on which design version you are making, follow the steps to add a neckband or hood.

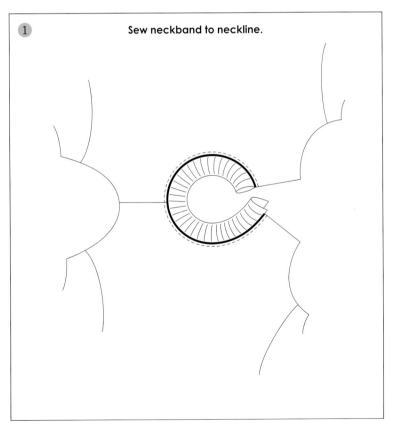

① Sew neckband to neckline.

For a Neckband

1 Press the neckband strip in half lengthwise, right side out. Align the cut edges of the band with the right side of the bodice neckline, and sew. Stretch the neckband gently as you sew so it curves nicely around the neck. Snip the threads and trim any excess neckband fabric at the end of the seam.

2 Sew the second shoulder seam, reinforcing it if necessary, and close the neckband. Press the neckband ends toward the front. Stitch a small triangular tack with straight stitches to hold this seam allowance in place.

3 Press the neckline seam allowance down and then topstitch it to the bodice body with a stretch stitch.

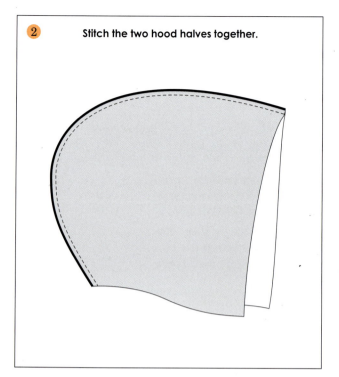

② Stitch the two hood halves together.

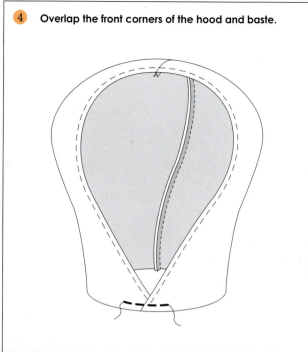

④ Overlap the front corners of the hood and baste.

For a Hood

1 Sew the second shoulder seam; reinforce it if you reinforced the first one.

2 Stitch the two hood halves together along the crown/back seam.

3 For an unlined hood, fold the hood hem allowance under twice, press, and topstitch. For a lined hood, stitch the lining pieces together along the crown/back seam. Place the hood and lining right sides together, aligning the crown seam and front edges, and sew along the front edge. Turn the hood right side out and press. Topstitch ½ inch (12 mm) from the edge. See the sidebar on page 67 for tips on making the hood stay up.

4 Overlap the front corners of the hood about 1¼ inches (3 cm). Baste the layers together.

5 Center the back of the hood on the bodice-back neckline and secure with a pin. Center the front of the hood on the bodice-front neckline and secure with a pin. Sew the hood to the neckline, stretching the hood to fit the neckline if necessary. Press down the seam allowance and topstitch with a stretch stitch, as desired.

AN ALTERNATIVE TO DRAWSTRINGS

Drawstrings pose a strangulation hazard, so they're not a good option for children's clothing. To be sure the hood stays up, add a bit of elastic at the front crown—that's usually enough to do the trick.

Cut a piece of ⅜-inch-wide (1 cm) elastic approximately 5 inches (13 cm) long. Before hemming the opening of the hood (or attaching the lining), align the elastic along the front seam allowance—or in the hem allowance for an unlined hood—centering it on the crown seam; pin at the center only. Stretch one half of the elastic and pin it to the hood edge. Do the same for the other half of the elastic.

With a stretch stitch, such as a three-step zigzag stitch, sew the elastic to the hood edge, stretching it to flatten the fabric as you stitch. Now complete the hood as usual.

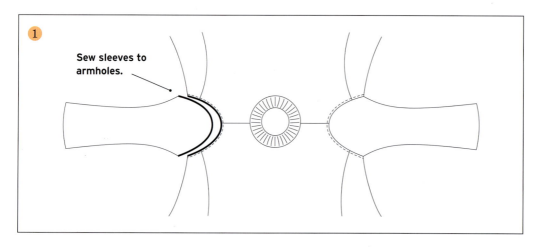

1

Sew sleeves to armholes.

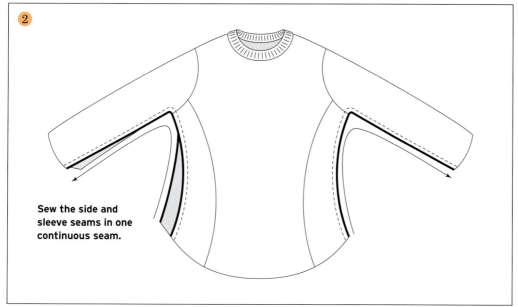

2

Sew the side and sleeve seams in one continuous seam.

tip!
The sleeve hem circumference can be pretty small on toddler-size shirts. If you're having trouble sewing the hems, try hemming the sleeves flat, before you sew the side and sleeve seams.

Attach the Sleeves and Sew the Side Seams

1 For a basic short or long sleeve, center the sleeve on the shoulder seam, aligning the sleeve-cap edge with the armhole edge; secure with pins. Sew the sleeve to the armhole. Repeat for the opposite sleeve. If you're using the fuller version of sleeve 7, see "Customize the Sleeves," on page 69.

2 On one side of the shirt, align the side seams and the sleeve underarm seams, and pin. Sew the side and sleeve seams in one continuous seam, beginning at the bodice hem. Repeat for the opposite side.

3 Fold the sleeve hem allowances under and press. Sew the hems with a stretch stitch.

4 Fold the shirt hem allowance under and sew with a stretch stitch.

CUSTOMIZE THE SLEEVES

Here are a few additional design options. You can make them working with the same pattern pieces. Just make a few adjustments as follows:

For the girl's fuller sleeve style (pattern piece 7), sew a short line of gathering stitches in the center of the sleeve-cap seam allowance. Pull the bobbin thread gently to draw up the sleeve so it fits the armhole. Attach the sleeve as described in step 1 on page 68.

For a short puffed sleeve, use pattern piece 8. Fold the hem allowance under ½ inch (1.3 cm) and topstitch with a straight stitch at ⅜ inch (1 cm), to form a casing. Attach the sleeves, as explained above, for a fuller sleeve. Cut a length of ¼-inch (6 mm)-wide elastic to fit the child's upper arm, plus 1 inch (2.5 cm). Insert the elastic into the casing and pin the ends at the seam allowances. Sew the sleeve and side seams as usual, catching the ends of the elastic in the seam.

For a layered look, cut both short and long sleeves; make sure the long sleeve isn't fuller than the short one. Hem both sleeves. Gather any sleeve caps that are cut from the fuller pattern. Lay the short sleeve, right side up, on the long sleeve's right side, with sleeve-cap edges aligned. Baste the layers together along the sleeve-cap edge. Treating the basted sleeves as a single unit, attach following step 1 on page 68.

For an athletic look, piece the sleeves to coordinate with pieced side panels. Use pattern piece 7, and cut the pattern apart along the marked line. Cut four of the undersleeve pattern from contrasting fabric. Join two undersleeves to each oversleeve (so that each sleeve comprises three pieces), then attach the sleeves as described on page 68.

tip!

Stretch fabrics require elasticized trims in any part of the garment that is subject to stretching. Nonstretch trims work in some areas, however—for example, down the length of the sleeve or horizontally across the shirt front.

APPLIQUÉ

Traditional appliqué features fabric cutouts arranged on a background cloth to create decorative motifs or patterns. Before you sew, you'll affix the cutouts to the cloth with paper-backed fusible web. Select the fusible with the least amount of adhesive that is still suitable for your fabric.

Step 1: On the paper side of the fusible web, draw or trace each of the shapes of the design you would like to appliqué. Draw each shape separately and, for less bulk, omit overlapping parts. The paper face will be the wrong side of the finished appliqué, so reverse any motifs that are not symmetrical.

Step 2: Fuse the fusible web, paper side up, to the wrong side of the appliqué fabric. If the fabric you're using for the appliqué tends to ravel, stabilize it with a featherweight fusible interfacing first.

Step 3: Cut out the appliqué shapes with the paper backing still attached.

Step 4: Prepare the fabric onto which you will appliqué. Heavy fabrics don't require stabilizing. Most other fabrics (and all knits) do. Interface just the area you'll be embellishing.

Step 5: Lay the base fabric pieces right side up. Remove the paper backing from the appliqué pieces and arrange them on the base. Then gently press them in place. If you're working with a lot of little pieces, lay a piece of parchment paper or a special Teflon-coated pressing cloth between the iron and the pieces to keep them in place.

Step 6: With the work right side up, sew the appliqué edges to the base fabric. I use a satin stitch. If the appliqué shapes overlap, sew the bottom layer pieces first. End each line of stitching with a few, very short, straight stitches. Cut the threads and tie off on the wrong side.

Instead of appliquéing directly onto a garment, you may arrange and sew the shapes onto a piece of felt. Then apply the felt to the garment like a decorative patch. Firm felt requires little or no stabilizing.

I like to create "rough" appliqués with fraying edges to give my projects some casual charm. Cut out each appliqué shape, but do not fuse it. Just affix it to the background fabric with pins or spray adhesive. As you sew, stitch a small distance in from the edge with a satin, straight, or decorative stitch. Then, if you like, snip the shape at intervals outside the stitching line to hasten the fraying.

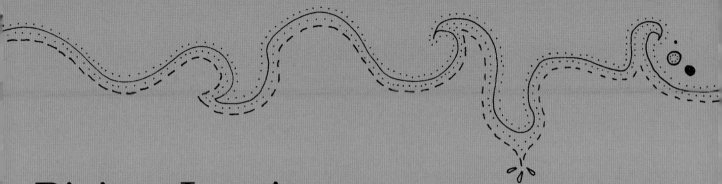

Riviera Leggings and Shorts

What's not to love about leggings? They're fun, fashionable, and comfortable. Girly-girls can climb trees, chase older brothers, play on the floor—all while wearing a skirt. Leggings are quick and easy to make. With just one pattern piece, you can sew your first pair in less than an hour, and the ones after that you'll surely be able to make in just thirty minutes or faster. Kids can never have too many pairs of leggings just for playing around in, but this pattern is great for activewear, too. Adjust the length to make cycling, dance, ice-skating, gymnastics, and swim wear that's both unique and much more affordable than ready-to-wear. In a super-soft cotton jersey, these leggings pair up with an Imke top for the snuggliest pajamas ever.

Recommended Fabrics:

- knit fabrics only, with 20% to 25% stretch across the grain
- 100-percent cotton or 98% cotton/2% Spandex-blend jersey
- interlock knits
- knit velour
- knit panné velvet

Notions

- 1-inch (2.5 cm)-wide sport elastic (which has channels to guide direct stitching onto garment), ¾ yard (70 cm)
- polyester sewing thread

Pattern Piece Cutting List: Pattern Sheet 3:

- *(11) Legging piece: Cut two (for shorts, cut at marked line).*

Sewing Riviera

Trace the Riviera pattern piece, if desired (page 36). Lay it on the fabric and cut (page 45), then transfer all the marks from the pattern to the fabric.

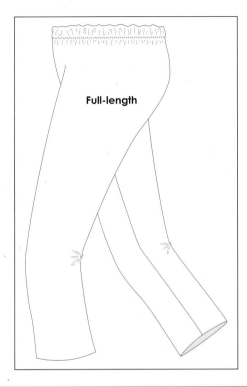

Full-length

note: Sew all seams with the fabric right sides together unless otherwise indicated. For construction seams, use a four-thread overlock stitch on a serger or a stretch stitch on a conventional machine. For topstitching, use a stretch stitch such as a three-step zigzag or a three-thread cover-stitch.

Size Chart

Size	18 mos.–2T 86/92		3T–4T 98/104		5T–6 110/116		7–8 122/128		9–10 134/140		11–12 146/152	
	US	EURO	**US**	EURO	**US**	EURO	**US**	EURO	**US**	EURO	**US**	EURO
Fully Extended Waist	**21¼"**	54 cm	**22"**	56 cm	**22⅞"**	58.5 cm	**23⅝"**	60 cm	**25¼"**	64 cm	**26¾"**	68 cm
Hip	**22⅞"**	58.5 cm	**23⅝"**	60 cm	**24⅜"**	62 cm	**25⅝"**	65.5 cm	**27¼"**	69 cm	**29½"**	75 cm
Side Length	**17"**	43 cm	**20½"**	52 cm	**24"**	61 cm	**27½"**	70 cm	**31⅛"**	79 cm	**34⅝"**	88 cm

HOW STRETCHY IS YOUR KNIT?

Tight-fitting clothes like leggings need plenty of give for comfort and longevity, so it's best to choose knit fabrics—but not all knits are the same. Evaluate your fabric before cutting and sewing, to ensure that the finished garment fits and wears well. A Spandex-cotton blend is a good choice for retaining shape and preventing saggy "elephant knees."

Start by checking the fabric's stretch. Fold the fabric across the grain (perpendicular to the selvage), and mark a 4-inch (10.7 cm) section on the fold. Grasp the ends of this section and stretch the fabric as far as you can. Measure the fully-stretched section. For leggings

or other close-fitting garments, the fabric should stretch at least 25 percent across the grain, or to a width of at least 5 inches (12.7 cm). If it doesn't, save the fabric for a looser-fitting garment. If it stretches much more than 25 percent—to 6 inches (15.2 cm) or more—cut the garment in a smaller size than indicated in the size chart, to avoid bagging.

Next, cut out a few fabric swatches that are about 8 inches (20.3 cm) square. Sew two swatches together along the grain, using the stitch recommended for your garment. Then sew two more together across the grain. Open the layers and pull in every

direction. The seams should stretch with the fabric (no popping stitches!), and the fabric shouldn't run or rip at the seamlines. Hold the stretched fabric up to the light and make sure you can't see through it. If you can see through it, use it for layered garments. Fabric that passes these tests is just right for Riviera, Imke (page 60), and Brooklyn (page 78). If you want to hem the legs with a stretch trim, sew a length of trim to the cross-grain swatch and check to make sure it stretches as much as the fabric—if it doesn't, your child won't be able to get her foot through the leg hem.

Fabric Requirements Table

Size	Fabric Width	18 mos.–2T 86/92		3T–4T 98/104		5T–6 110/116		7–8 122/128		9–10 134/140		11–12 146/152	
		US	EURO	US	EURO	US	EURO	US	EURO	US	EURO	US	EURO
Leggings	54" (140 cm)	⅝ yd	50 cm	¾ yd	60 cm	¾ yd	70 cm	⅞ yd	80 cm	1 yd	90 cm	1⅛ yd	100 cm

Amount required to make the entire full-length garment in one fabric.

Sew the Legs

1   Press the hem allowance of the leggings upward and topstitch. If desired, you can add stretch trim to the hem, or use the trim in place of a folded hem. Cut the trim the length of the hem circumference and apply it using the same stretch stitch as for the hem.

2   On one leg piece, align the inseams and sew. Repeat for the second leg.

3   Turn one leg right side out and insert it into the other leg, right sides together and with the crotch edges aligned. Sew the crotch seam.

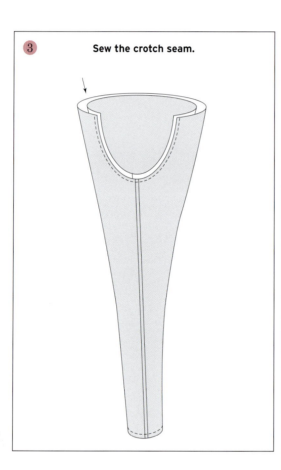

3   Sew the crotch seam.

RUCHING

A ruche (pronounced *roosh*) is a narrow, gathered strip of fabric, lace, or ribbon applied to the surface of a garment or other item. It's often referred to as ruching (*rooshing*). A ruche is similar to a ruffle but is always fairly narrow. It may be gathered on one or both long edges or along the center, and is often applied in a meandering pattern. Ruching can be cut on the straight grain, but it's really pretty when cut on the bias. Here's how to make a ruche that is gathered along the center.

Step 1: Decide how long you want the ruche to be. Cut a strip of fabric about three times that length and 1¼ to 1½ inches (3 to 4 cm) wide. Piece several strips together to the get the length you need.

Step 2: Finish both long edges of the strip with a narrow topstitched hem or a serger-rolled edge. If you want more texture, finish the edges with a small, wide, zigzag stitch and allow the material to fray. This technique works best when the fabric strip is cut on the bias and works especially well with twills.

Step 3: Sew two lines of gathering stitches along the center of the strip, spacing them a scant ⅛ inch (3 mm) apart.

Step 4: At one end of the ruche, firmly pull the bobbin and upper threads and tie the threads into a knot. Trim the excess thread. The knotting will pull the corners of the strip in toward each other and make a rounded end. Sew the two halves of the end together invisibly by hand from the wrong side.

Step 5: Pin the knotted-thread end of the ruche in place on your garment and gently pull the bobbin threads to gather the strip, pinning into position as you go. Sew along the center of the ruche with a straight or zigzag stitch.

Step 6: Trim any excess ruching and finish the end as you did the beginning.

Attach the Waistband

1 Measure your child's waist and cut a piece of 1-inch (2.5 cm)-wide sport elastic approximately 3 inches (7.5 cm) shorter than her waist measurement. Join the ends of the elastic with short zigzag stitches, to form a ring.

2 Divide and pin-mark the elastic in four equal sections; repeat for the leggings waistline. Pin the elastic ring to the inside of the leggings at the waist edge, aligning it with the waist edge and matching the pin marks. Place the elastic seam at center back.

3 Sew the elastic to the leggings waist with an overlock or a zigzag stitch. Stretch the elastic to fit the waistline as you sew, but don't stretch the leggings fabric. Remove the pins as you approach them.

4 Fold the elastic and the leggings fabric to the leggings wrong side and pin at the front, back, and sides. Press the folded fabric edge with a steam iron for good measure. Topstitch from the right side with one or two lines of a stretch stitch to secure the elastic. Again, stretch the elastic as you sew.

tip!
Add a small loop of ribbon under the elastic at the back waist to help your child distinguish the front from the back when dressing.

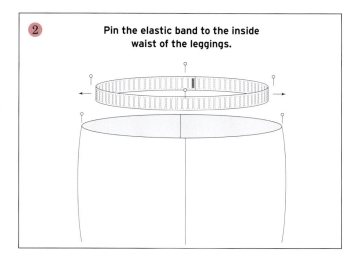

2 Pin the elastic band to the inside waist of the leggings.

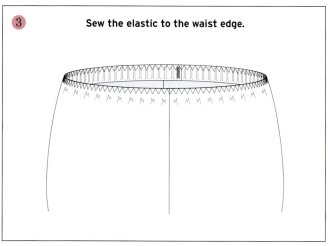

3 Sew the elastic to the waist edge.

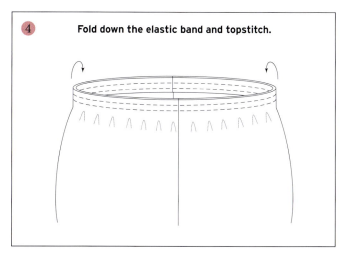

4 Fold down the elastic band and topstitch.

Brooklyn Tank Top

The Brooklyn Tank Top is a quick and (if you have a knack for knits) very easy project. You can make this little top with straps that tie at the shoulders, or you can make it with straps that join the front and the back like a girls' undershirt, which is a better method if you plan to layer the tank under other pieces. Regardless of the type of strap you choose, select fabrics that are tightly knit, so the straps don't stretch too much lengthwise and fall off the shoulders. Note that this top takes only about ¾ yard (69 cm) of fabric, so you can squeeze one out of your small remnants.

Recommended Fabrics:

- knit fabrics only, with 20% to 25% stretch across the grain (page 75)
- 100% cotton or 98% cotton/2% Spandex-blend jersey
- interlock knits
- knit velour
- knit panné velvet

Notions

- polyester sewing thread

Pattern Piece Cutting List: Pattern Sheet 5

- *(9) Front:* Cut one on the fold.
- *(10) Back:* Cut one on the fold.
- *(11) Trim for front:* Cut one.
- *(12) Trim for back:* Cut one.
- *(13) Shoulder straps:* Cut two (cut longer piece for tied straps, shorter piece for regular straps).

Sewing Brooklyn Tank Top

Select the appropriate pattern pieces for your garment, and trace them if desired (page 36). Lay the pieces on the fabric and cut them (page 45). Take special care when cutting the straps—they need to be long enough and an even width. Transfer all the marks from the pattern to the fabric.

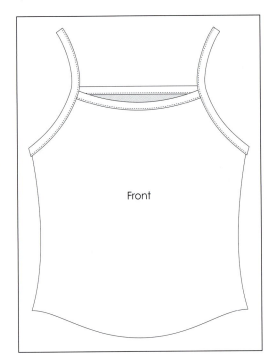

Front

note: *Sew all seams with the fabric right sides together unless otherwise indicated. For construction seams, use a four-thread overlock stitch on a serger or a stretch stitch on a conventional machine. For topstitching, use a stretch stitch, such as a three-step zigzag or a three-thread cover-stitch.*

Size Chart

Size	18 mos.–2T 86/92		3T–4T 98/104		5T–6 110/116		7–8 122/128		9–10 134/140		11–12 146/152	
	US	EURO	US	EURO	US	EURO	US	EURO	US	EURO	US	EURO
Fully Extended Waist	21¼"	54 cm	22"	56 cm	22⅞"	58.5 cm	23⅝"	60 cm	25¼"	64 cm	26¾"	68 cm
Hip	22⅞"	58.5 cm	23⅝"	60 cm	24⅜"	62 cm	25⅝"	65.5 cm	27¼"	69 cm	29½"	75 cm
Side Length	17"	43 cm	20½"	52 cm	24"	61 cm	27½"	70 cm	31⅛"	79 cm	34⅝"	88 cm

1 Align one long edge of the front trim along the upper edge of the shirt front and sew. Repeat for the shirt back and back trim.

2 Fold the front trim over the front upper edge and toward the shirt wrong side; press. The free edge of the trim should lie just below the first stitching line. Topstitch the folded trim from the right side with a stretch stitch, catching the free edge on the wrong side in the topstitching. Cut excess trim from the ends of the trim band. Repeat this step for the shirt back. If you are making tie straps, proceed to page 82. If you are making plain straps, skip to page 83.

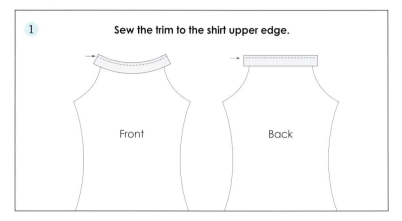

1 **Sew the trim to the shirt upper edge.**

Front

Back

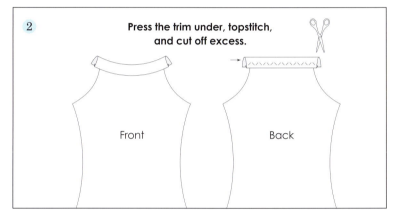

2 **Press the trim under, topstitch, and cut off excess.**

Front

Back

Fabric Requirements Table

Size	Fabric Width	18 mos.–2T 86/92		3T–4T 98/104		5T–6 110/116		7–8 122/128		9–10 134/140		11–12 146/152	
		US	EURO	US	EURO	US	EURO	US	EURO	US	EURO	US	EURO
Top	54" (140 cm)	⅝ yd	50 cm	¾ yd	60 cm	¾ yd	70 cm	⅞ yd	80 cm	1 yd	90 cm	1 ⅛ yd	100 cm

Amount required to make the entire garment in one fabric.

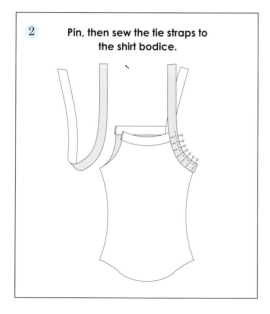

2 Pin, then sew the tie straps to the shirt bodice.

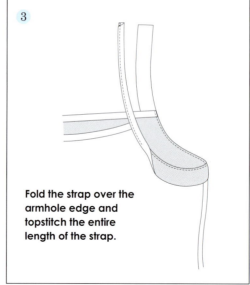

3 Fold the strap over the armhole edge and topstitch the entire length of the strap.

tip!

If you want, you can cut the straps and front and back trim pieces from woven fabric. Cut strips of fabric on the true bias (45 degrees to the selvage), slightly more than three times as wide as you want the finished trim and straps. If you're making plain straps, pin and fit them before sewing so they're just the right length.

For Tied Straps:

1 Sew the bodice back and front together along the side seams.

2 Center one tie strap on one side seam, right sides together. Align the strap's raw edge with the armhole edge and pin in place, as shown above. Sew the strap to the bodice, using a seam allowance of ⅛ to ¼ inch (3 to 6 mm). Repeat for the other strap.

3 Fold the free edge of the strap over the armhole edge to the inside, as you did for the front and back trim, and press. Continue folding the strap into thirds along its free section, press, and pin to secure. If desired, tuck the strap ends between the layers for a more finished look. Sew along the entire length of the strip or bias tape. Repeat for the opposite armhole. Go to step 2 under "Finishing."

BROOKLYN BIKINI TOP

To make a Brooklyn bikini top, shorten the tank bodice as desired. Sew the hem as a ¾-inch (2 cm)-wide casing, leaving a 1-inch (2.5 cm) opening. Cut a piece of ½-inch (1.3 cm)-wide elastic to fit the child's chest. With a safety pin or bodkin, insert the elastic into the hem casing. Join the ends of the elastic with short zigzag stitches. Push the elastic join into the casing and close the opening with a stretch stitch.

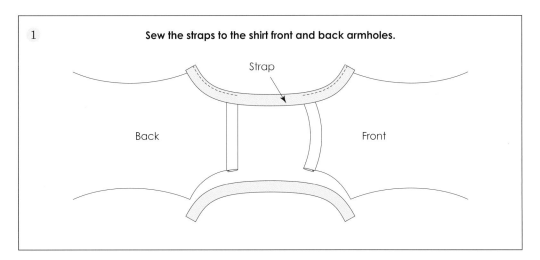

1 Sew the straps to the shirt front and back armholes.

Strap

Back

Front

tip!
If your fabric is especially stretchy, cut the shoulder straps 1 to 2 inches (2 to 5 cm) shorter than the pattern length.

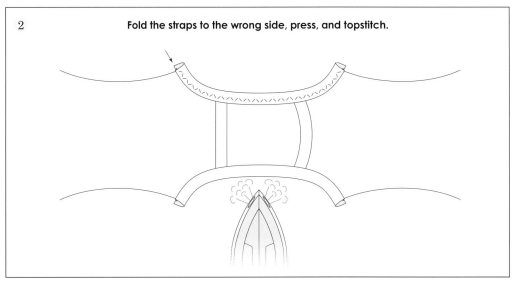

2 Fold the straps to the wrong side, press, and topstitch.

For Plain Straps

1 Lay the shirt front and back, right side up, as shown above. Referring to the illustration, position the end of one strap along one underarm of the front, right sides together. Sew it to the front piece. Position the free end of the strap strip along the shirt back in the same way and sew. Repeat for the opposite strap.

2 Fold the strap over the edge of the fabric and to the inside. Continue this fold along the shoulder portion of the strap, folding it in thirds. Press, then pin. Beginning at one side seam,

topstitch the entire length of the strap. If the fabric raw edge is visible along the shoulder portion, trim close to the stitching. Repeat for the opposite shoulder strap.

Finishing

1 Align the shirt side seams and sew.

2 Fold the hem allowance under and topstitch.

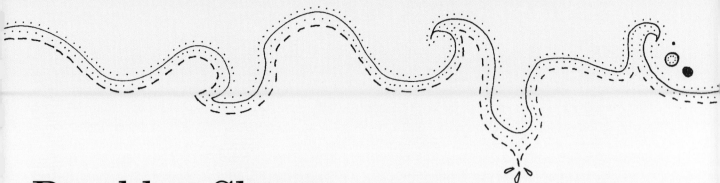

Brooklyn Shrug

This quick-to-sew, mini cardigan is perfect for warding off summer evening breezes, blasts of air conditioning, and even the bright rays of the sun on delicate shoulders. As you can see at left, the Brooklyn Shrug also works as an elegant cover-up to complement the sleeveless Manhattan dress on page 130. The Brooklyn Shrug and the Brooklyn Tank Top are each incredibly versatile and work perfectly well alone or in combination. Mix, match, and layer these two garments made in all types of knits to create outfits that go from the beach, to the playground, to a special holiday party.

Recommended Fabrics:

- knit fabrics only, with 20% to 25% stretch across the grain (page 75)
- 100% cotton or 98% cotton/2% Spandex-blend jersey
- interlock knits
- Polar fleece
- knit velour
- knit panné velvet

Notions

- polyester sewing thread

Pattern Piece Cutting List: Pattern Sheet 3

- (8) Front piece: Cut two.
- (9) Back piece: Cut one on the fold.
- (10) Sleeve: Cut two on the fold.

Sewing Brooklyn Shrug

Select the appropriate pattern pieces for your garment, and trace them if desired (page 36). Lay the pieces on the fabric and cut them (page 45). Transfer all the marks from the pattern to the fabric.

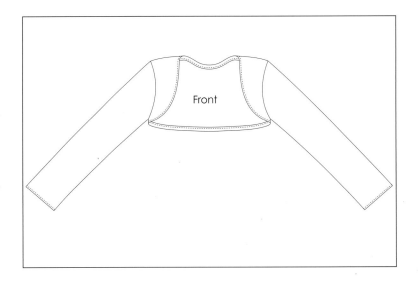

Front

note: *Sew all seams with the fabric right sides together unless otherwise indicated. For construction seams, use a four-thread overlock stitch on a serger or a stretch stitch on a conventional machine. For topstitching, use a stretch stitch, such as a three-step zigzag or a three-thread coverstitch.*

Size Chart

Size	18 mos.–2T 86/92		3T–4T 98/104		5T–6 110/116		7–8 122/128		9–10 134/140		11–12 146/152	
	US	EURO	**US**	EURO	**US**	EURO	**US**	EURO	**US**	EURO	**US**	EURO
Chest	**19¾"**	50 cm	**23⅝"**	60 cm	**24½"**	62 cm	**26"**	66 cm	**27½"**	70 cm	**30¾"**	78 cm
Shoulder Width	**2¼"**	5.5 cm	**2¼"**	5.5 cm	**2⅜"**	6 cm	**2½"**	6.5 cm	**2⅞"**	7 cm	**3⅜"**	8.5 cm
Sleeve Length	**11⅝"**	29.5 cm	**13¼"**	33.5 cm	**14⅝"**	37 cm	**16¾"**	42.5 cm	**18¾"**	47.5 cm	**20⅝"**	52 cm

Fabric Requirements Table Amount required to make the entire garment in one fabric.

Size	Fabric Width	18 mos.–2T 86/92		3T–4T 98/104		5T–6 110/116		7–8 122/128		9–10 134/140		11–12 146/152	
		US	EURO	**US**	EURO	**US**	EURO	**US**	EURO	**US**	EURO	**US**	EURO
Shrug	**54"** (140 cm)	½ yd	40 cm	½ yd	40 cm	½ yd	45 cm	⅝ yd	50 cm	¾ yd	55 cm	¾ yd	60 cm

1 Sew the fronts to the back at the shoulders.

2 Sew the sleeves to the bodice.

3 Fold the sleeve hem allowances under and topstitch.

4 Sew the sleeve and side seam on each side of the shrug in one continuous action.

5 Fold under the neckline, front, and bodice hem edges; press and topstitch.

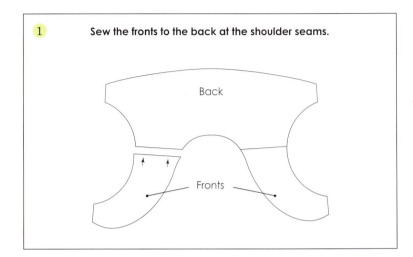

1 **Sew the fronts to the back at the shoulder seams.**

Back

Fronts

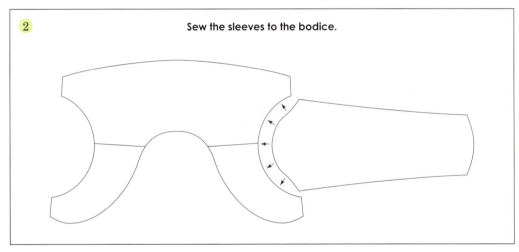

2 **Sew the sleeves to the bodice.**

tip!
Some decorative machine stitches stretch well and look nice, too. Experiment with these stitches to create a pretty hem and edge treatment.

5 **Press the body edges under and topstitch.**

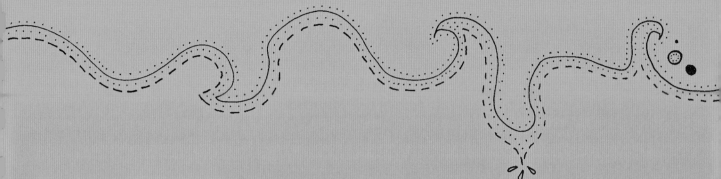

Insa Skirt

Insa is easy and fast to sew, but offers lots of opportunities for embellishment and personalization—so you can make it as simple or as elaborate as you and your child like. Insa is a two-layer skirt with a yoke and an elasticized waistline. The yoke provides a streamlined fit around the waist and hips, so it works well with overblouses and tees. The flared gores make the skirt perfect for leaping and twirling. Add vertical gathers to the overskirt gores for a textured, romantic look. Although Insa is delightful in a solid color, it begs to be made in a creative, colorful mix of fabrics, with trims, ruffles, appliqué, embroidery, or all of the above. This skirt is a modern classic, which you will sew for your girl from the time she is a bubbly toddler until she is a spunky tween.

Recommended Fabrics:

- light- to medium-weight cotton and cotton-blend percales, corduroy, velvet, taffeta
- overksirt may be sewn of organza or tulle for a special occasion.

Notions

- 1-inch (2.5 cm)-wide elastic for the waistband, one piece the size of the child's waist plus 1 inch (2.5 cm)
- ¼-inch (6 mm)-wide elastic for the elastic gathers (optional), about 4 yards (3.7 meters)
- sewing thread

Pattern Piece Cutting List: Pattern Sheet 2

- (1) Overskirt gore: Cut four.
- (2) Underskirt gore: Cut four.
- (3) Yoke: Cut one on the fold.
- Waistband (optional): Cut a strip 5 inches (13 cm) wide and as long as the yoke waistline circumference plus a seam allowance.

Sewing Insa

Before cutting your fabric, decide which fabrics you want to use where on the skirt. Plan the trim placement, too—you may need to apply some trims during construction rather than after the skirt is finished. Sketch your design (page 52), select the appropriate pattern pieces for your garment, and trace them if desired (page 36). Lay the pieces on the fabric and cut them (page 45), then transfer all the marks from the pattern to the fabric.

note: *Sew all seams with right sides together, unless otherwise indicated. For construction seams and topstitching, use a straight stitch. Finish all seam allowances with a three-thread overlock stitch or a zigzag stitch. Unless otherwise indicated, topstitch through the garment and all layers of the seam allowances, ⅛ inch (3 mm) or ¼ inch (6 mm) from the seamline. The heavier the fabric, the farther from the seam you should place the topstitching line.*

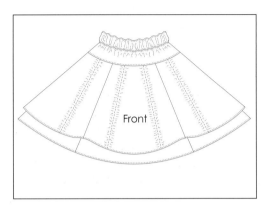

Size Chart

Size	18 mos.–2T 86/92		3T–4T 98/104		5T–6 110/116		7–8 122/128		9–10 134/140		11–12 146/152	
	US	EURO	US	EURO	US	EURO	US	EURO	US	EURO	US	EURO
Fully Extended Waist Circumference	23 ⅝"	60 cm	24 ⅜"	62 cm	25 ¾"	65.5 cm	27 ⅛"	69.0 cm	29 ¾"	75.5 cm	32 ⅞"	83.5 cm
Length	12 ⅝"	32 cm	14 ½"	37 cm	16 ½"	42 cm	18 ½"	47 cm	20 ½"	52 cm	23 ¼"	59 cm

Construct the Skirts

1 Finish the right and left edges of all the skirt gore pieces before sewing the seams. Sew the underskirt pieces right sides together. Press the seam allowances open, and topstitch along both sides of each seam.

2 If you want vertical gathers on the overskirt gores, add them now, following the instructions for "gathering with elastic" on page 92. Then sew the overskirt pieces together. If desired, insert piping or other trim in the seams during this part of construction. Press the seam allowances open and topstitch along both sides of the seam. If you want trim on the skirt gores or along the seams, apply it now, before attaching the yoke.

3 Pin the overskirt wrong side to the underskirt right side along the waist edge, then baste the skirts together along the top edge.

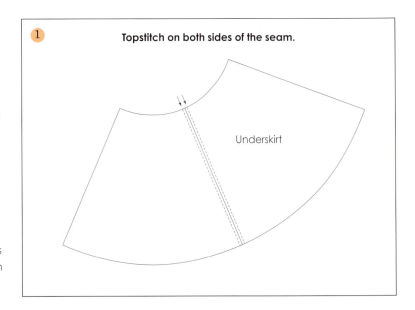

① Topstitch on both sides of the seam.

Underskirt

tip!

For perfectly parallel topstitching, install a twin needle and sew both rows of stitching in a single pass.

Fabric Requirements Table

Size	Fabric Width	18 mos.–2T 86/92		3T–4T 98/104		5T–6 110/116		7–8 122/128		9–10 134/140		11–12 146/152	
		US	EURO	US	EURO	US	EURO	US	EURO	US	EURO	US	EURO
Fabric for Overskirt and Yoke Only	54" (140 cm)	⅜ yd	41 cm	¾ yd	69 cm	⅞ yd	80 cm	1 yd	91 cm	1 yd	91 cm	1⅜ yd	126 cm
Fabric for Underskirt Only	54" (140 cm)	⅜ yd	41 cm	⅝ yd	69 cm	¾ yd	80 cm	⅞ yd	80 cm	1⅛ yd	103 cm	1¼ yd	114 cm

This chart shows how much fabric is needed to make the skirt in two fabrics: one for the yoke and overskirt, the other for the underskirt. If making the skirt in one fabric only, add the amounts.

Attach the Yoke

1 Sew the yoke piece into a ring, right sides together. Make certain the yoke and the skirt waist circumferences match. If necessary, open one yoke seam, adjust, and restitch. Press the seam allowances open and topstitch along both sides of the seam.

2 Pin the yoke to the skirt unit. Center the seam of the yoke on the back of the skirt waist. Sew the yoke to the skirt waist through all layers, press up the seam allowances, and topstitch.

GATHERING WITH ELASTIC

A few strips of elastic sewn along the overskirt gores work magic. They add texture and shape that are a little reminiscent of a fairy-tale princess dress! To create the gathers, cut equal pieces of ¼-inch (6 mm)-wide elastic one-quarter to one-third shorter than the elastic placement lines on the overskirt pieces. The longer the elastic, the softer the gathers.

Pin the elastic pieces to the wrong side of the overskirt gores along

the placement lines, anchoring them at the hem edge and the yoke edge. Set the sewing machine for a long, narrow three-step or a regular zigzag stitch. Take a few stitches to anchor one end of an elastic strip to the skirt. Then, as you sew, pull the elastic to match the length of the placement line. Stitch the length of the elastic, then backstitch to secure the end. Repeat for the remaining elastic pieces.

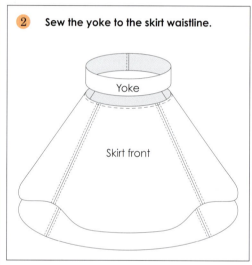

2 Sew the yoke to the skirt waistline.

Yoke

Skirt front

Pin elastic at top and bottom of placement lines. Sew with a zigzag stitch.

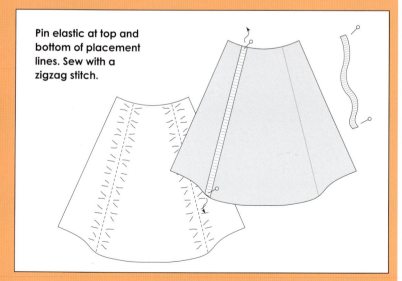

Complete the Waistband and Hems

1 For a fold-over casing, follow these three steps. For a separate waistband casing, see the directions at right. Form the casing by folding the upper edge of the yoke 1⅝ inch (4 cm) to the wrong side. Edgestitch ⅛ inch (3 mm) from the fold.

2 Sew a line approximately ¼ inch (6 mm) from the raw edge of the fabric. Leave a 1½-inch (4 cm) opening for inserting the elastic. Cut a strip of 1-inch (2.5 cm)-wide elastic to fit the child's waist plus 1-inch (2.5 cm). Working with a safety pin or bodkin, insert the elastic into the opening in the casing, around the waist, and out the opening. Join the ends of the elastic by overlapping them and sewing with short zigzag stitches. Tuck the elastic into the opening in the waistband and close the opening with straight stitches.

3 Fold the underskirt hem allowance under twice, press, and pin. Topstitch along the inner fold to secure the hem. Repeat for the overskirt. Add trims and ruffles to embellish the hems, if desired.

ADDING A SEPARATE WAISTBAND

Instead of a fold-over casing at the waist, you can opt to add a separate waistband— it's a perfect place to incorporate a contrasting fabric. Start by trimming 1 inch (2.5 cm) off the yoke's upper edge. Cut a waistband strip, referring to the pattern piece cutting list (page 89). Then simply follow the instructions for sewing and attaching the Dortje waistband (page 103). The waistbands for these two garments are exactly the same!

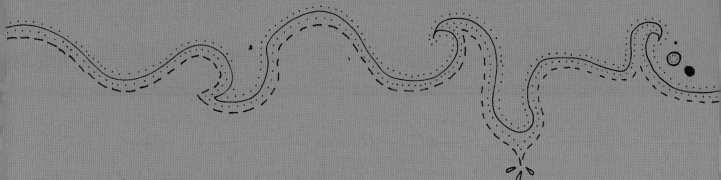

Dortje Trousers

The Dortje Trousers design is a pair of trousers that really fits and flatters! The silhouette grows with the girl. This year's back-to-school long pants look great at Capri length by summer break, and the elasticized waistband is comfortable in every season. Design-wise, Dortje offers almost limitless possibilities. You can bring in plenty of playful contrast by piecing the legs along the horizontal seams, or keep the colors monochromatic to emphasize the sweetly flared shape. Add ruching on the leg or ruffles at the cuffs and in horizontal seams for an extra-feminine touch. Or keep the pants simple for très chic style.

Recommended Fabrics:

- bottom-weight cotton or cotton/Spandex-blend twills, corduroys, velvets, light- to medium-weight denims, sailcloth, sturdy percale

Notions

- ¼-inch (6 mm)-wide elastic for elastic gathers (optional), about one yard
- 1-inch (2.5 cm)-wide elastic for waistband, one piece the size of the child's waist plus 1 inch (2.5 cm)
- sewing thread

Pattern Piece Cutting List: Pattern Sheet 1

For solid, unpieced pants:

- (9) Front pant leg: Cut two.
- (10) Back pant leg: Cut two.

For pieced pants, cut apart pieces 9 and 10 along the marked lines, then cut as follows:

- (9) Upper-front piece: Cut two.
- (9) Front knee piece: Cut two.
- (9) Lower-front piece: Cut two.
- (10) Upper-back piece: Cut two.
- (10) Back knee piece: Cut two.
- (10) Lower-back piece: Cut two.

For all pants:

- (11) Front-pocket bag: Cut two.
- (12) Front-pocket facing: Cut two.
- (13) Rear-pocket piece: Cut two.
- (14) Waistband: Cut one on the fold.

Sewing Dortje

Before cutting your fabric, decide whether you want a plain or pieced pant leg. Sketch your design (page 52), select the appropriate pattern pieces for your garment, and trace them if desired (page 36). Lay the pieces on the fabric and cut them (page 45), then transfer all the marks from the pattern to the fabric.

Size Chart

Size	18 mos.–2T 86/92		3T–4T 98/104		5T–6 110/116		7–8 122/128		9–10 134/140		11–12 146/152	
	US	EURO	US	EURO	US	EURO	US	EURO	US	EURO	US	EURO
Fully Extended Waist Circumference	24"	61 cm	24¾"	56 cm	25½"	65 cm	26¾"	68 cm	28"	71 cm	30"	76 cm
Hip	24½"	61.5 cm	25½"	60 cm	26¾"	68 cm	29"	73.5 cm	31½"	80 cm	34"	86.5 cm
Length at Side Seam (without gathers)	16⅜"	42 cm	19⅞"	52 cm	23"	59.5 cm	26¼"	66.5 cm	30½"	77.5 cm	33¾"	85.5 cm

Front

Back

note: Sew all seams with right sides together, unless otherwise indicated. For construction seams and topstitching, use a straight stitch. Finish all seam allowances with a three-thread overlock stitch or an overcast zigzag stitch. Unless otherwise indicated, topstitch through the garment and all layers of the seam allowances, ⅛ inch (3 mm) or ¼ inch (6 mm) from the seamline. The heavier the fabric, the farther from the seam you should place the topstitching line.

Fabric Requirements Table

Size	Fabric Width	18 mos.–2T 86/92		3T–4T 98/104		5T–6 110/116		7–8 122/128		9–10 134/140		11–12 146/152	
		US	EURO	US	EURO	US	EURO	US	EURO	US	EURO	US	EURO
Trousers	54" (140 cm)	1⅛ yd	90 cm	1⅛ yd	100 cm	1¼ yd	110 cm	1⅜ yd	120 cm	1⅜ yd	130 cm	1½ yd	140 cm

Amount required to make the entire garment in one fabric.

Make and Attach the Pockets

1 Lay one pocket facing on an upper-front piece, aligning the pocket opening edges. Sew along the opening edge. Repeat this step for the opposite pocket.

2 Trim and/or clip the seam allowance, then turn the pocket facing to the inside and topstitch.

3 Pin the front-pocket bag piece to the front-pocket facing along the bottom and inner side edges. Sew along this edge and finish the seam allowances. Repeat this step for the opposite front pocket.

4 Finish all the rear-pocket piece edges. Fold the pocket side and bottom allowances to the wrong side and press. Topstitch along the folded edges, ¼ inch (6 mm) from the edge.

5 Fold the upper edge of the rear pockets under twice and press. Edgestitch along this fold at ¼ inch (6 mm) and again at ⅛ inch (3 mm).

6 Position the rear pockets on the marks on the upper-back pieces and secure with a few pins. Sew along the side and bottom edges of each pocket at ⅛ inch (3 mm). Secure the upper corners with bar tacks sewn with a zigzag stitch set at a narrow width and short stitch length.

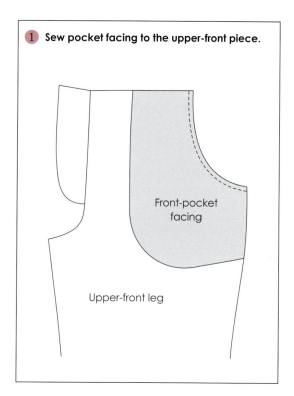

1 Sew pocket facing to the upper-front piece.

Front-pocket facing

Upper-front leg

tip!

Before you topstitch the pockets to the pant backs, apply a strip of fusible-web tape to the side and bottom edges of each pocket. Position the pockets on the pants and press them in place. The pockets will stay right where you put them while you stitch!

GATHERING THE KNEE PIECES

You can vary the pant leg silhouette by adding gathers to the knee pieces—especially charming on toddler-sized trousers. Here's what to do:

Step 1. Cut four pieces of ¼-inch (6 mm)-wide elastic approximately one-quarter to one-third shorter than the length of the side edges of the back-knee piece. For heavy, hard-to-gather fabrics, opt for a longer strip of elastic.

Step 2. Pin one end of an elastic strip to the side of one back-knee piece, on the right side of the fabric and aligned with the fabric edge, so the entire width of the elastic is within the seam allowance. Set the machine for a three-step zigzag stitch. Place the back-knee piece and the pinned elastic end under the presser foot, and sew a few stitches. Continue sewing, stretching the elastic along the seam allowance until it reaches the opposite end of the back-knee piece. Be sure to keep the elastic strip completely within the seam allowance.

Step 3. Repeat step 2 for the remaining three side edges of the back-knee pieces.

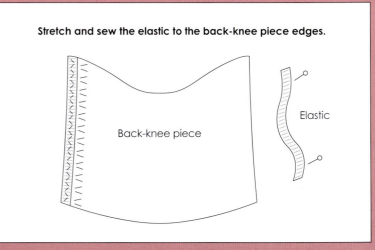

Stretch and sew the elastic to the back-knee piece edges.

Back-knee piece

Elastic

Assemble the Pant Legs

1 If making unpieced pants, skip to step 4 below. If you plan to gather the knee pieces, do so now, referring to the sidebar on page 99. If you want to include piping, ruffles, or trim in the piecing seams, do that now. (See page 113 for instructions on making ruffles.)

2 Sew the upper-front piece to the front-knee piece. Press up the seam allowances and topstitch. Sew the lower-front piece to the front-knee piece. Press up the seam allowances and topstitch. Repeat for the other front pant leg.

3 Sew the upper-back piece to the back-knee piece, press up the seam allowances, and topstitch. Stitch the lower-back piece to the back-knee piece, press up the seam allowances, and topstitch. Repeat for the other back pant leg.

4 Pin the front pocket bags to the pant front, with their sides aligned along the side seams. Sew one pant front to the corresponding pant back along the side seam, catching the pocket side in the seam. Press the seam allowances toward the back and topstitch. Repeat for the other pant leg.

5 On one pant leg, align the inseam raw edges. Sew the inseam, and press the seam allowances toward the front. If you want to topstitch this seam, position the pant leg over the sewing machine's free arm. Or, for a cleaner line, instead of using the free arm to topstitch, scrunch the pant leg behind the presser foot—almost turning it inside out—as you sew. Repeat this step for the opposite pant leg.

6 Fold the hem allowances under twice and topstitch. Or add ruffles or trim to finish the pant hem.

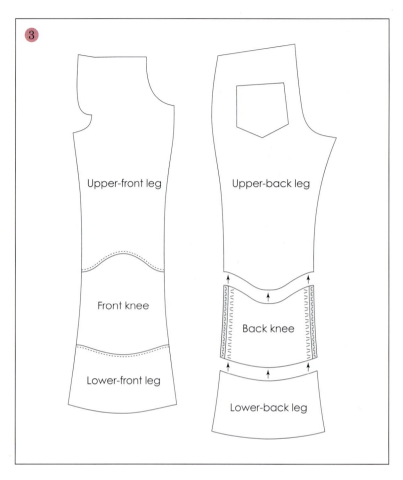

③

Upper-front leg

Upper-back leg

Front knee

Back knee

Lower-front leg

Lower-back leg

tip!

If you've included elastic gathers at the knees, you need to stretch the elastic as you complete the side and inseams. For all construction seams, finishing, and topstitching, stretch the elastic so that the back-knee piece is fully extended and its seamline matches the front-knee piece seamline. Sew finishing stitches and topstitching right over the elastic.

Construct a Faux Fly

1 Turn one pant leg right side out. Place it inside the other leg, right sides together and crotch seam edges aligned. Pin, then sew, the seam.

2 Turn the pants right side out. Tuck the fly extensions in to form a little vertical pocket. Press the fly extensions and the entire crotch seam to one side and pin.

3 With a marking tool, mark a stitching line on the outside of the pants that follows the line of the fly extensions underneath and mimics the topstitching of a zipper fly. Beginning at the front waist edge, stitch along this marked line, then topstitch from the bottom of the faux fly up to the back waist edge, ⅛ inch (3 mm) from the seam. If you'd like, add a zigzagged bar tack at the base of the faux fly to make it appear more like a zipper fly.

1 Place one pant leg inside the other and sew the crotch seam.

Fly extensions

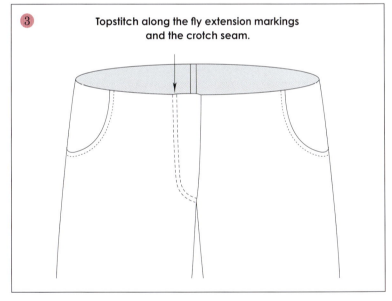

3 Topstitch along the fly extension markings and the crotch seam.

Attach the Waistband

1 Sew the short ends of the waistband together to form a ring, leaving a ½-inch (1.3 cm) opening in the stitching line for inserting the elastic, as shown in the drawing.

2 Aligning the short waistband seam with the pants center-back seam, pin the waistband to the pants waistline, waistband right side to the pant wrong side. Position the waistband so that the elastic opening is closer to the waist edge. Sew the waistband to the pant waist edge.

3 Press the waistband up, and fold it on the marked fold line toward the garment right side. Press the fold line and edgestitch ⅛ inch (3 mm) from the fold. Fold the free, raw edge of the waistband under ¼ inch (6 mm) and press. Pin this edge to the pants and topstitch through all layers to secure it.

4 Cut a length of 1-inch (2.5 cm)-wide elastic to fit the child's waist, plus 1 inch (2.5 cm). Working with a safety pin or bodkin, insert the elastic through the opening in the waistband, pull it around the waistband and out the opening. Secure the ends of the elastic by overlapping them and sewing with short zigzag stitches. Tuck the elastic inside the opening and close the opening with a few hand stitches.

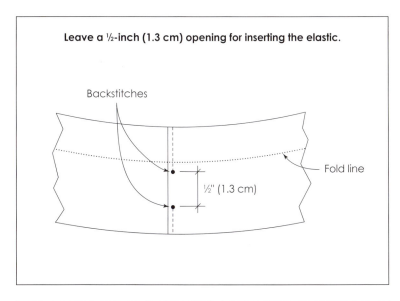

Leave a ½-inch (1.3 cm) opening for inserting the elastic.

Backstitches

Fold line

½" (1.3 cm)

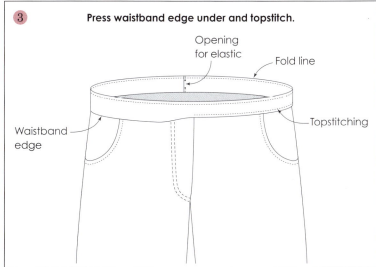

3 **Press waistband edge under and topstitch.**

Opening for elastic

Fold line

Topstitching

Waistband edge

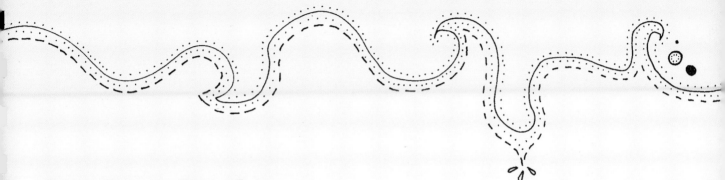

Avalon Jacket

The Avalon Jacket is named for the city on Catalina Island—just a short ferry ride and yet worlds away from the concrete canyons of Los Angeles. I made this jacket to experiment with petal forms that create a rippling hem edge. Sewing this pattern, you'll see how a dramatically curved, vertical seamline creates a horizontal wave—the hemline makes this jacket a real head-turner. The pretty and playful silhouette pairs beautifully with Dortje (page 94), Insa (page 88), Feliz (page 122), and Manhattan (page 130). This pattern works in monochromatic and multi-colored schemes. If you can't choose between versions, put two styles into a single garment by making the jacket fully reversible (page 111).

Recommended Fabrics:

- cotton percale, corduroy, medium-weight twill, sweat-shirt fabric, Polar fleece, taffeta

Notions

- buttons or snaps
- fusible interfacing
- sewing thread

Pattern Piece Cutting List: Pattern Sheet 2

- (4) Center-front piece: Cut two.
- (5) Side-front piece: Cut two.
- (6) Center-back piece: Cut one on the fold.
- (7) Side-back piece: Cut two.
- (8) Back-neck facing: Cut one on the fold.
- (9) Front-neck facing: Cut two.
- (10) Sleeve: Cut two.

Sewing Avalon

Start by selecting the appropriate pattern pieces for your garment, and trace them if desired (page 36). Lay the pieces on the fabric and cut them (page 45), then transfer all the marks from the pattern to the fabric.

Size Chart

Size	18 mos.–2T 86/92		3T–4T 98/104		5T–6 110/116		7–8 122/128		9–10 134/140		11–12 146/152	
	US	EURO	US	EURO	US	EURO	US	EURO	US	EURO	US	EURO
Chest	28"	71 cm	28¾"	73 cm	29½"	75 cm	31⅛"	79 cm	32⅝"	83 cm	35¾"	91 cm
Shoulder Width	3⅛"	8 cm	3¼"	8.5 cm	3⅜"	9 cm	3⅝"	9.5 cm	3⅞"	10 cm	5⅛"	10.5 cm
Front Length	15⅛"	38.5 cm	16¾"	42.5 cm	18¼"	46.5 cm	19⅞"	50.5 cm	21½"	54.5 cm	23⅞"	60.5 cm
Sleeve Length	13½"	34.5 cm	15"	38 cm	16⅝"	42.5 cm	18⅝"	47.5 cm	20½"	52 cm	22½"	57 cm

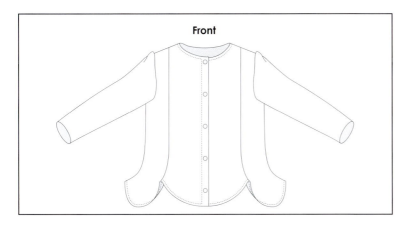

Front

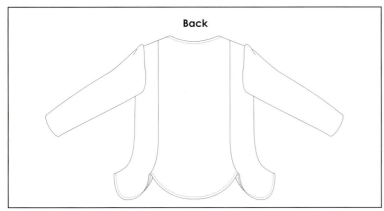

Back

note: *Sew all seams with right sides together, unless otherwise indicated. For construction seams and topstitching, use a straight stitch. Finish all seam allowances with a three-thread overlock stitch or a zigzag stitch. Unless otherwise indicated, topstitch through the garment and all layers of the seam allowances, ⅛ inch (3 mm) or ¼ inch (6 mm) from the seamline. The heavier the fabric, the farther from the seam you should place the topstitching line.*

Fabric Requirements Table

Size	Fabric Width	18 mos.–2T 86/92		3T–4T 98/104		5T–6 110/116		7–8 122/128		9–10 134/140		11–12 146/152	
		US	EURO	US	EURO	US	EURO	US	EURO	US	EURO	US	EURO
Jacket	54" (140 cm)	1⅛ yd	90 cm	1⅛ yd	100 cm	1¼ yd	105 cm	1⅜ yd	120 cm	1⅜ yd	130 cm	1½ yd	140 cm

Amount required to make the entire garment in one fabric.

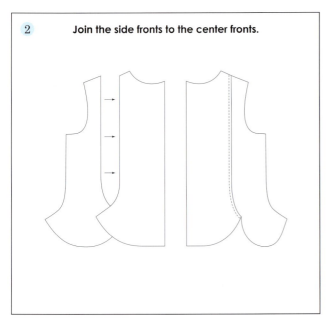

2   Join the side fronts to the center fronts.

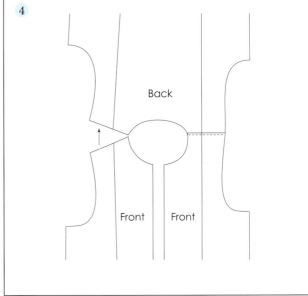

4

Back

Front   Front

Sew the Bodice

1 Apply a strip of fusible interfacing to the wrong side of the front facings on each center-front piece, to support the closures.

2 Sew the center-front pieces to the side-front pieces. Press the seam allowances toward the center and topstitch at ⅛ inch (3 mm).

3 Sew the center-back piece to the side-back pieces. Press the seam allowances toward the center and topstitch at ⅛ inch (3 mm) on both sides of the seam.

4 Sew the jacket fronts to the back at the shoulder seams. Press the seam allowances toward the front of the jacket and topstitch at ¼ inch (6 mm).

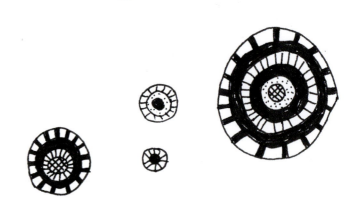

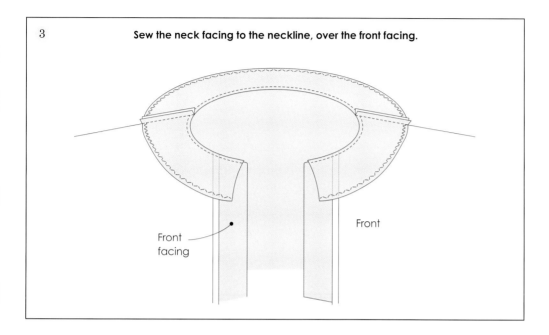

3   **Sew the neck facing to the neckline, over the front facing.**

Front
facing

Front

Attach the Neck Facings

1   Sew the front-neck facing pieces to the back-neck facing piece. Press the seam allowances open and, if desired, topstitch the seams on both sides of the seam. Finish the outside edge of the neck facing with an overlock or zigzag stitch, or by turning under the edge and topstitching.

2   Press the raw edges of the front facings toward the garment wrong side approximately ⅛ to ¼ inch (3 to 6 mm). Now, fold the front facings to the right side along the marked fold line and pin. Pin the neck facing to the neckline, right sides together, aligning the shoulder seams and allowing the neck facing to overlap the front facing. The front facing folded edge should extend ¼ inch (6 mm) beyond the ends of the neck facing. Sew the neck facing to the neckline, catching the folded-back front facings in the seam.

3   Trim and clip the neckline seam allowances and clip the front corners at an angle. Turn the neck and front facings to the garment wrong side. Press the neckline seam and the front facing fold line. Edgestitch around the neckline at ⅛ inch (3 mm).

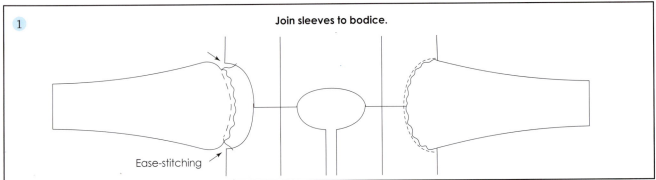

1 Join sleeves to bodice.

Ease-stitching

Attach the Sleeves and Complete the Side Seams

1 Sew a line of long straight stitches between the sleeve cap marks. Pin the sleeve cap to the armhole, with raw edges aligned, pulling the bobbin thread to gather the sleeve cap slightly to fit. Sew the armhole seam, then press the seam allowances toward the bodice and topstitch at ⅛ inch (3 mm).

2 On one side of the jacket, align the side seams and the sleeve underarm seam, and pin. Sew the sleeve and side seams in a continuous action. Repeat for the other side. Press the side seam allowances toward the front and topstitch at ⅛ inch (3 mm).

TWO JACKETS IN ONE!

It's easy to make the Avalon Jacket fully reversible—and it won't take much more time than sewing an unlined version. Start by trimming the front facing strip from the center-front pattern piece, leaving a seam allowance. Then, cut the center- and side-front pieces, center- and side-back pieces, and sleeves from both the outer and the inner jacket fabrics. Omit the neck facings. Assemble both jacket bodices (minus facings) and attach the sleeves as shown on page 110. Because all the seam allowances are hidden inside the jacket, there's no need to finish them.

Step 1: To join the inner and outer jackets, pin them right sides together along the center fronts and neck edges. Sew this seam, then trim and clip the seam allowances as needed. Turn the jacket right side out, and press the edges.

Step 2: Sew together the sleeve hems, as follows: Insert the inner sleeves inside the outer sleeves and align the sleeve seams at the hem. Safety-pin the seams together at each sleeve hem. Reach into the sleeve, between the two sleeve layers,

through the open hem of the jacket between the inner and outer jacket bodices. Grasp the two sleeves at the safety pin and draw the pinned sleeve hems through the sleeve and out through the open bottom of the jacket. Ignore the crumpled jacket body—just focus on the sleeve hems.

Step 3: Remove the safety pin but keep the inner and outer sleeve seams aligned. The two sleeve hems now face each other, like the ends of two joined pipes. Fold the inner and outer sleeve hems out slightly and pin them right sides together. Sew around this circular hem. Reinsert the inner sleeve into the outer sleeve and pull the sleeves back through the garment and into place. Repeat the process for the opposite sleeve.

Step 4: Turn the whole jacket inside out through the open hem. Pin the hem layers, right sides together. Sew the hem closed, leaving a 4-inch (10 cm) opening at the center back. Turn the jacket right side out through this opening. Tuck in the seam allowances of this opening and press the hem edge. Sew closed by hand.

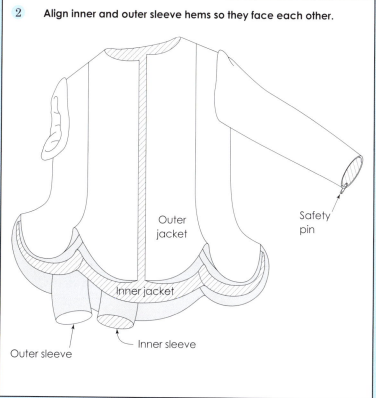

2   **Align inner and outer sleeve hems so they face each other.**

Outer jacket

Inner jacket

Safety pin

Outer sleeve

Inner sleeve

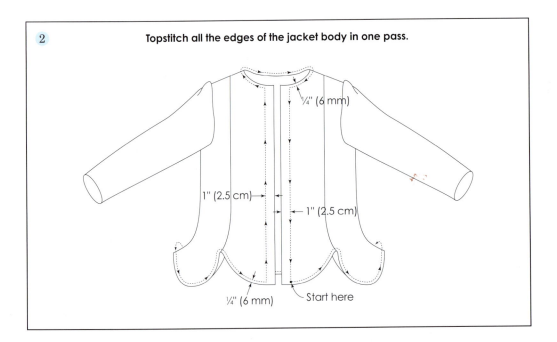

(2) **Topstitch all the edges of the jacket body in one pass.**

¼" (6 mm)

1" (2.5 cm)

1" (2.5 cm)

¼" (6 mm)

Start here

Sew the Hem and Add Closures

1 Fold the hem allowance under twice. Press. Pin in place.

2 Starting at the lower front corner and sewing in a continuous line, topstitch the hem, front facings, and the neckline, as shown in the illustration above.

3 Fold the sleeve hem allowances under twice and topstitch.

4 Add closures. You can use buttons and buttonholes, snaps, Velcro dots, or your own creative variation. Mark the spacing for the closures carefully on each side of the front. Apply the closures.

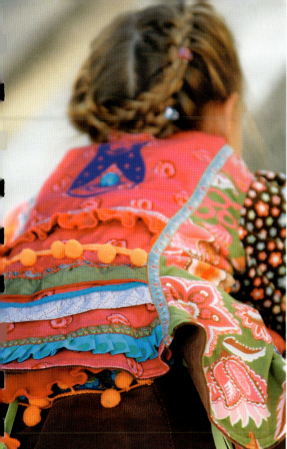

GATHERED RUFFLES

Ruffles, especially long ones, take a bit of patience, but they're charming, and little inconsistencies in the gathering will never be noticed. You can cut strips for ruffles across the width of your fabric (the most economical option) or on the lengthwise grain.

Step 1: Measure the part of the garment where you would like to add a ruffle. For a very full ruffle, cut a strip of fabric three times as long as your measurement. For a ruffle with less volume, cut the strip twice as long. If necessary, sew several strips together to get the right length.

Step 2: If the ruffle is going to extend all the way around the garment, sew the ends together to make a ring. If you're not sure how full you want the ruffle to be, leave the ends unjoined until you've pinned it to the garment and adjusted the fullness to have the effect you want.

Step 3: Finish the bottom edge of the ruffle, either with a narrow topstitched hem or with a serger-rolled edge.

Step 4: Gather the top edge (page 49). Place the piece to which the ruffle will be sewn right side up. Then put the ruffle right side down on top, aligning the gathered ruffle edge with the garment edge. Pin the fabrics together at even intervals. Sew the pieces together, stitching just below the gathering threads.

To apply a ruffle on top of your garment like a trim, position the ruffle right side up on the right side of the garment. Sew on the ruffle and then cover the gathered edge with a piece of ribbon or another decorative element.

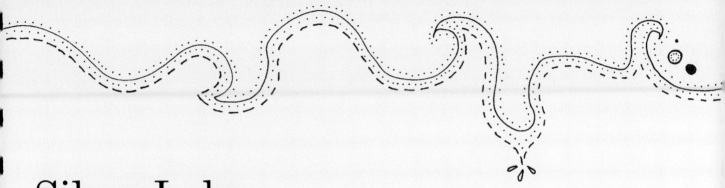

Silver Lake Windbreaker

Silver Lake is where the not-yet-discovered creative community in Los Angeles congregates. It's an easygoing, life-is-good, no-time-like-the-present kind of place, dotted with edgy shops and relaxing cafés. With the same low-key-with-a-twist vibe, the Silver Lake windbreaker is a casual, functional piece for both boys and girls. This zippered windbreaker (shown with snaps in the photo at left) recalls a 1950s-style blouson jacket, but the classic style is updated with some spunky pieced panels, four (yes, four!) pockets, and a cool, handy media pocket on the sleeve for technology-toting tots. Silver Lake is designed to be fully lined, so it can just as easily be made fully reversible to do double-duty. If you want, you can, of course, omit the lining entirely.

Recommended Fabrics:

- Shell and reversible side: waterproof nylon, percale, tweed, medium-weight cotton twills
- Lining: similar light- to medium-weight fabrics, Polar fleece for the bodice; nylon knit or woven for the sleeves
- Pockets and pocket linings: lighter-weight fabrics

Notions

- separating zipper (use length specified in Fabric Requirements Table; if making a reversible jacket, use a reversible zipper)
- fusible interfacing
- sewing thread

Pattern Piece Cutting List: Pattern Sheet 5

- *(1) Jacket front:* Cut two each from shell fabric and lining or reverse-side fabric.
- *(2) Jacket back:* Cut one each on the fold from shell fabric and lining or reverse-side fabric.
- *(3) Back yoke:* Cut one each on the fold from shell fabric and lining or reverse-side fabric.
- *(4) Side panels:* Cut four each from shell fabric and lining or reverse-side fabric.
- *(5) Pocket:* Cut four each from pocket outer fabric and pocket lining fabric (if making a reversible jacket, cut an additional four each of the reverse-side pocket outer and lining fabrics).
- *(6) Collar:* Cut two on the fold from shell fabric or cut one each from shell and reverse-side fabrics.
- *(7) Sleeve:* Cut two each from shell fabric and lining or reverse-side fabric.
- *(8) Media pocket on sleeve:* Cut one from pocket outer fabric and one from pocket lining fabric. (If making a reversible jacket, cut an additional one each of the reverse-side pocket outer fabric and reverse-side pocket lining fabric.)

Sewing Silver Lake

Before cutting your fabric, make a few design decisions and sketch the garment (page 52). Plan how many pockets you want and decide whether you want them in contrasting or self-fabric. Consider piecing the jacket bodice along the curved panel seams.

Select the appropriate pattern pieces for your garment, and trace them if desired (page 36). Lay the pieces on the fabric and cut them (page 45), then transfer all the marks from the pattern to the fabric. For a reversible jacket, cut additional pocket pieces for the reverse side.

Size Chart

Size	18 mos.–2T 86/92		3T–4T 98/104		5T–6 110/116		7–8 122/128		9–10 134/140		11–12 146/152	
	US	EURO	US	EURO	US	EURO	US	EURO	US	EURO	US	EURO
Chest	31½"	80 cm	32½"	82.5 cm	33"	84 cm	34⅝"	88 cm	36¼"	92 cm	39⅜"	100 cm
Shoulder Width	3¼"	8.5 cm	3⅜"	9 cm	3½"	9 cm	3¾"	9.5 cm	4"	10 cm	4¼"	11 cm
Front Length	15¾"	40 cm	17⅜"	44.5 cm	18¾"	47.5 cm	20¼"	51.5 cm	21¾"	55 cm	24"	61 cm
Front Length	12⅜"	31.5 cm	14⅛"	36 cm	15⅞"	40.5 cm	17¾"	45 cm	19½"	49.5 cm	21½"	54.5 cm

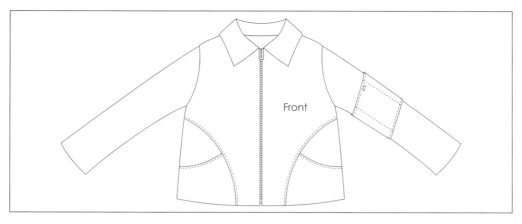

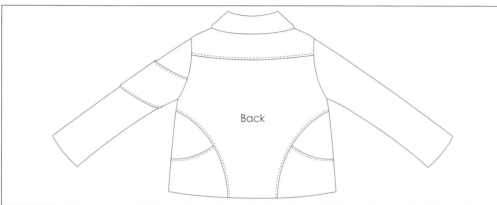

note: *Sew all seams with right sides together, unless otherwise indicated. For construction seams and topstitching, use a straight stitch. For a lined jacket, there is no need to finish the seam allowances. Unless otherwise indicated, topstitch through the garment and all layers of the seam allowances, ⅛ inch (3 mm) or ¼ inch (6 mm) from the seamline. For basting, use a straight stitch set for a long stitch length, and remove basting stitches after sewing the final seam. The instructions are for a basic lined jacket, but include variations for a reversible jacket. Read through before beginning so you know which steps apply to your project.*

Fabric Requirements Table

Size	Fabric Width	18 mos.–2T 86/92		3T–4T 98/104		5T–6 110/116		7–8 122/128		9–10 134/140		11–12 146/152	
		US	EURO	US	EURO	US	EURO	US	EURO	US	EURO	US	EURO
Jacket	54" (140 cm)	1 ⅜ yd	120 cm	1 ⅜ yd	125 cm	1 ⅜ yd	130 cm	1 ½ yd	135 cm	1 ½ yd	145 cm	1 ⅝ yd	155 cm
Zipper Length		10"	25 cm	12"	30 cm	14"	35 cm	16"	40 cm	18"	45 cm	20"	50 cm

Amount needed for shell or lining; double the amount if making lining and shell from one fabric.

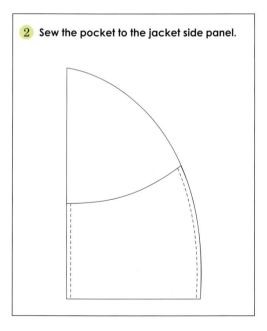

2 Sew the pocket to the jacket side panel.

Make the Bodice Pockets

1 Pin one pocket-lining piece to one pocket-outer piece, with the upper edges aligned. Sew along the top pocket edge. Turn the pocket lining to the inside, and press the seam. Edgestitch along the seam at ⅛ inch (3 mm) and again at ¼ inch (6 mm). Repeat for the remaining pockets. (Reversible option: Make reverse-side pockets in the same way.)

2 Pin each pocket to a jacket side panel, with the pocket lining against the side panel right side. Align the bottom and side edges. Sew along the two sides and the bottom, ⅛ inch (3 mm) from the edge. (Reversible option: Repeat for reverse-side pockets.)

Sew the Outer and Lining Bodices

1 On the outer and inner jackets, sew the side-front panels to the center front pieces. Press the seam allowances toward the center front, but do not topstitch.

2 On the outer and inner jackets, sew the side back panels to the center-back piece. Press the seam allowances toward the center back, but do not topstitch.

3 On the outer and inner jackets, sew the shoulder yoke piece to the jacket outer back piece, right sides together. Press the seam allowance upward and topstitch at ⅛ inch (3 mm).

4 On both the inner and the outer jackets, sew the jacket fronts to the jacket backs at the shoulders. Press the seam allowances toward the front and topstitch.

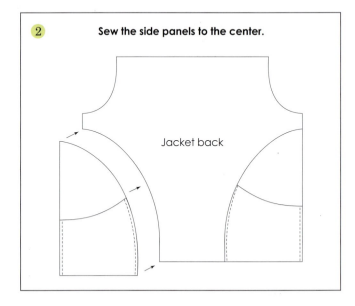

2 Sew the side panels to the center.

Jacket back

Attach the Sleeves
and Sew the Side Seams

1 Attach the media pocket(s), referring to the sidebar on page 121.

2 Sew the outer sleeves to the outer jacket. Repeat for the lining or reverse-side jacket.

3 Lay the outer jacket inside out and align the side seams and sleeve seams; pin. Sew the side seam and sleeve seam on one side of the jacket in one continuous motion, then repeat for the other side. Sew the sleeve/side seams of the lining or reverse-side jacket the same way.

4 Press the side seam allowances open, and topstitch along both sides of the side seam at ⅛ inch (3 mm).

5 Topstitch along the back side-panel seam from the back hem to the side seam, and continue from the side seam along the front side-panel seam to the hem in one continuous arc. Repeat this topstitching for the opposite side, then for the lining or reverse-side jacket.

Insert the Zipper

1 Install a zipper foot on your machine. Separate the two sides of the zipper and pin the zipper tapes to the outer jacket front edges as shown. Align the bottom zipper stop approximately ⅝ inch (1.6 cm) from the bottom edge. The top tape ends should extend to the neckline.

2 Sew the zipper tapes to the jacket fronts, keeping the stitching line approximately ¼ inch (6 mm) from the teeth.

tip!
Instead of pinning to sew, baste the zipper tape to the jacket by hand or position it with a strip of wash-away basting tape. Either method keeps the zipper flatter than pinning does.

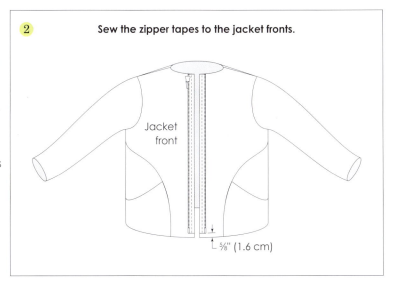

② Sew the zipper tapes to the jacket fronts.

Jacket front

⅝" (1.6 cm)

Attach the Collar

1 Install a standard presser foot on your machine. Pin the upper and under collar pieces together. Sew along the outer edges. Trim the seam allowances.

2 Turn the collar right side out and gently push the corners out with a point turner. Press, then edgestitch around the collar at ⅛ inch (3 mm).

3 Place the under collar and outer jacket right sides together. Align the neckline edges and center backs and baste.

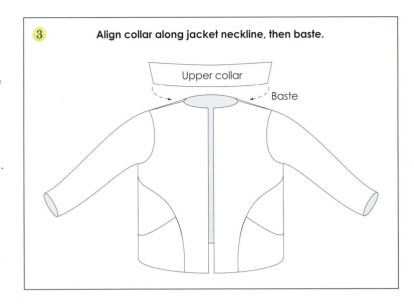

3 Align collar along jacket neckline, then baste.

Upper collar

Baste

Install the Lining

1 Place the lining or reverse-side jacket right sides together over the outer jacket with center-front edges aligned; pin the front edges. Install a zipper foot on your machine. Sew through all layers along one side of the zipper, stitching ⅛ inch (3 mm) away from the zipper teeth. Repeat for the other side of the zipper.

2 Place the lining to the outer jacket around the neckline, sandwiching the neck edge of the collar between the two layers. Carefully fold the top zipper tape ends at right angles and pin between the lining and outer jacket. Sew all the way around the neckline. Trim the seam allowance and turn. Press the seam but do not topstitch. To sew the sleeve and bottom hems, follow steps 2 through 4 in "Two Jackets in One!" on page 111.

3 Press the edges of the opening inward and, beginning at the point marked in the illustration, edgestitch along the jacket hem. Continue topstitching up along one zipper side of the jacket, around the neckline, and down the opposite zipper side until you reach the starting point.

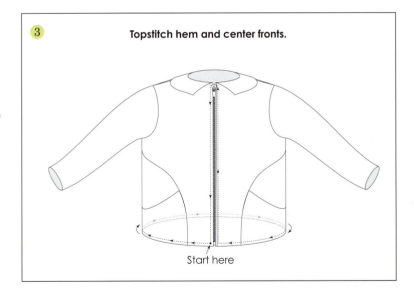

3 Topstitch hem and center fronts.

Start here

tip!
Make a loop to hang the jacket by inserting a loop of ribbon about 4 inches (10 cm) long in the seam between the jacket collar and the lining.

POCKET FOR GEAR

This media pocket encircles the wearer's upper arm and stores whatever electronics (or other small stuff) your child likes to tote.

Step 1. Pin the media pocket lining to the media pocket piece at the long edges, and sew. Turn this tube right-side-out and press the seams. Edgestitch along the upper edge at ⅛ inch (3 mm) and again at ¼ inch (6 mm).

Step 2. Sew a small piece of hook-and-loop tape to the lining side of the media pocket between the marks. Lay the pocket on the sleeve, aligning the upper curved corner with the armhole seam.

Mark the placement for the opposite side of the hook-and-loop tape on the sleeve, then sew the tape in place.

Step 3. Position the media pocket on the sleeve at the marks and pin. Edgestitch the lower edge of the media pocket to the sleeve at ⅛ inch (3 mm) and again at ¼ inch (6 mm).

Step 4. With a marking tool and straightedge, mark three vertical lines on the pocket to divide it into sections that fit your media. Sew along the marked lines with a straight stitch. You can use a twin needle to stitch two parallel lines at each mark.

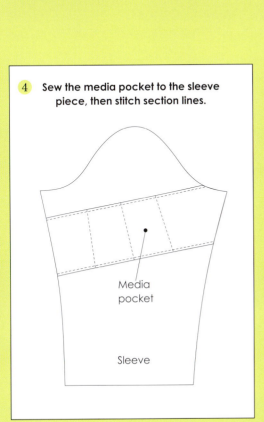

4   **Sew the media pocket to the sleeve piece, then stitch section lines.**

Media pocket

Sleeve

Feliz Party Dress

Feliz is the Spanish word for "happy," but this happy dress was named for the Los Feliz district of Los Angeles. During the early years of the Golden Age of Hollywood, many movie studios called Los Feliz home. This part of town is retro and modern in equal doses, just right for a dress that can be anything you want it to be. Feliz is a clever, two-layer dress. The full-skirted underdress is topped with a shorter, pinafore-style overdress that's open in the back. An elasticized panel at the center back provides comfort and room to grow, and ties cinch the raised waist for a custom fit. Omit the shoulder straps, and the dress can be worn at waist level as a skirt. Layer Feliz over a T-shirt or blouse, pop a shrug over it, or pull on leggings underneath.

Recommended Fabrics:

- cotton percale, voile, batiste, fine-wale corduroy, light-weight denim and twill, linen, taffeta, and organza

Notions

- ⅝-inch (1.5 cm)-wide elastic, approximately 18 inches (46 cm)
- ribbons for button loops (optional), approximately 9 inches (23 cm) or more for larger buttons
- buttons (optional)
- ribbon for sash (optional, if using ribbon instead of fabric sash), approximately 2¾ yards (2.5 meters)
- fusible interfacing
- sewing thread

Pattern Piece Cutting List: Pattern Sheet 3

- (1) Shoulder-strap front piece: Cut four (two fronts, two facings).
- (2) Shoulder-strap back piece: Cut four (two backs, two facings).
- (3) Overdress front piece: Cut one on the fold (note "Cut here for overdress" line).
- (4) Overdress side piece: Cut two on the fold (note "Cut here for overdress" line).
- (3) Underdress front/back piece: Cut two on fold.
- (4) Underdress side piece: Cut two on fold.
- (5) Underdress back-facing piece: Cut one on fold.
- (6) Sash piece: Cut two on the fold.
- (7) Overdress side-facing pieces (optional; use facings if including button loops): Cut two.

Sewing Feliz

Lay out your fabrics and plan your design. Decide which fabrics to use for which layers, and how you want to embellish the dress. Make a sketch to use as a guide while you sew (page 52). Select the appropriate pattern pieces for your garment, and trace them if desired (page 36). Lay the pieces on the fabric and cut them (page 45), then transfer all the marks from the pattern to the fabric.

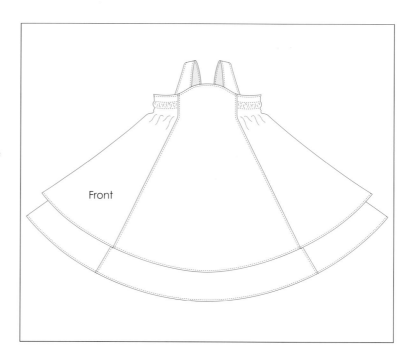

Front

Size Chart

Size	18 mos.–2T 86/92		3T–4T 98/104		5T–6 110/116		7–8 122/128		9–10 134/140		11–12 146/152	
	US	EURO	US	EURO	US	EURO	US	EURO	US	EURO	US	EURO
Chest Circumference	23⅝"	60 cm	24⅜"	62 cm	25¼"	64 cm	26¾"	68 cm	28¾"	72 cm	31½"	80 cm
Shoulder Width	1⅝"	4.0 cm	1¾"	4.5 cm	1¾"	4.5 cm	1¾"	4.5 cm	1⅞"	4.7 cm	2⅛"	5.2 cm
Front Length	21¼"	54 cm	23⅝"	60 cm	26"	66 cm	29½"	75 cm	33"	84 cm	37⅜"	95 cm

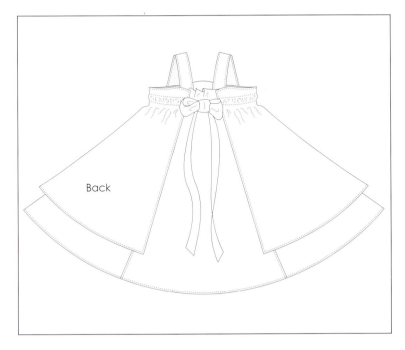

Back

note: *Sew all seams with right sides together, unless otherwise indicated. For construction seams and topstitching, use a straight stitch. Finish all seam allowances with a three-thread overlock stitch or a zigzag stitch. Unless otherwise indicated, topstitch through the garment and all layers of the seam allowances, ⅛ inch (3 mm) or ¼ inch (6 mm) from the seamline. The heavier the fabric, the farther from the seam you should place the topstitching line. For basting, use a straight stitch set for a long stitch length. Remove basting stitches after sewing the final seam.*

Fabric Requirements Table

Size	Fabric Width	18 mos.–2T 86/92		3T–4T 98/104		5T–6 110/116		7–8 122/128		9–10 134/140		11–12 146/152	
		US	EURO	US	EURO	US	EURO	US	EURO	US	EURO	US	EURO
Overdress	54" (140 cm)	1 yd	95 cm	1⅛ yd	100 cm	1¼ yd	110 cm	1⅜ yd	120 cm	1½ yd	140 cm	1¾ yd	155 cm
Underdress	54" (140 cm)	1⅛ yd	105 cm	1¼ yd	110 cm	1⅝ yd	120 cm	1⅝ yd	130 cm	1½ yd	150 cm	1⅞ yd	165 cm

Fabric requirements are given separately for the overdress and the underdress. If you want to make the dress entirely from one fabric, add the overdress and underdress requirements together.

Prepare the Sash and Button Loops

1 Apply fusible interfacing to the seam allowance wrong sides at the sash placement marks on the side panels of the overdress.

2 Fold each sash piece lengthwise, right sides together, and sew across the pointed end and along the long edge. Trim the seam allowance corners. Turn the sashes right side out, pushing the pointed corner out with a chopstick or other tool. Press the sashes with the seam along one edge. Edgestitch around the entire sash at ⅛ inch (3 mm).

3 If you are including buttons on the back of the dress, apply fusible interfacing to the wrong side of the overdress side facings. If you're not using buttons, you may omit the side-facing pieces.

4 You can form optional button loops from folded ribbon. Experiment with the ribbon and buttons to determine how large to make the loops; be sure to leave ends long enough to include in the facing seam (see step 2 under "Sew the Overdress").

DESIGN TIPS FOR FELIZ

• Feliz's simple piecing enables fabricoholics to combine four or more different prints easily and prettily. If you want to combine fabrics, first assess their compatibility. Fabrics and trims should share care requirements. You'll have best results combining fabrics and trims of similar weights within each garment layer. To keep the dress comfortable and inviting to wear, offset a heavy layer with a lighter one.

• If you want to embellish the under- and overdresses (and why wouldn't you?) plan the embellishment scheme ahead. Many decorative treatments are easier to apply to a flat pattern piece than to a finished garment. Use your sketch to note what goes where—and when. Designing is a little like engineering and well worth the effort when a special dress comes together just the way you want it.

• If you are making a Feliz skirt, match your child's waist measurement to the corresponding chest measurement on the size chart.

• You can substitute a ribbon—or a handful of assorted pretty ribbons—for the fabric sashes if desired. Cut two ribbon sashes the length of the sash pattern piece. Trim one end of each ribbon on the diagonal to prevent fraying. Attach the ribbons as you would a fabric sash.

Add a piece of elastic to the open end of each sash.

Elastic

BUILT-IN DRESSING EASE

I recommended adding a bit of elastic where the sashes join the overdress. This elastic remains hidden between the over-and underdress layers, but enables the child to dress and undress without undoing the sash.

Trim 3 or 4 inches (7 to 10 cm) from the open ends of each sash piece. Cut two pieces of elastic 2 to 3 inches (5 to 7 cm) long. Insert one end of an elastic strip into the open end of a sash piece and sew it securely with a short zigzag stitch. Repeat the process for the other sash. Attach the sash pieces to the overdress as described in step 1 below.

Sew the Overdress

1 Lay the overdress front flat, right side up. Lay one overdress side piece on top, right-side-down and raw edges aligned. Lay one sash piece on top of the side piece, with its open end (or elastic) aligned with the overdress side seam at the sash placement mark. Pin; then sew all layers. Repeat for the opposite side and sash. The sashes should now be attached to the overdress wrong side. Press the seam allowances toward the front and topstitch at ⅛ inch (3 mm).

2 If you're not using side facings, fold the over-dress side edges under twice and topstitch to secure. If you're using side facings and button loops, pin the loops to one side edge of the overdress, right sides together. Position one button loop above the sash and the rest below the sash, spacing them about 1 inch (2.5 cm) apart—or as needed to accommodate the size of your button. Pin the overdress side facings to the overdress side pieces and sew, catching the button loops in the seam. Turn the facings under and press.

3 Fold the hem allowance under twice, press, and topstitch. If you have used side facings, edgestitch the overdress sides now.

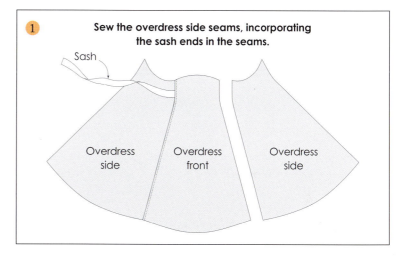

1 Sew the overdress side seams, incorporating the sash ends in the seams.

Sash

Overdress side

Overdress front

Overdress side

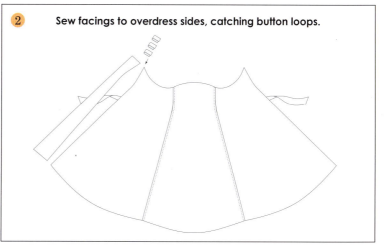

2 Sew facings to overdress sides, catching button loops.

1 Sew the back facing to the underdress back.

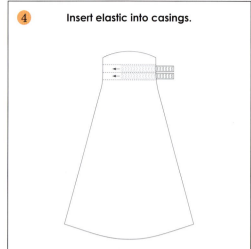

4 Insert elastic into casings.

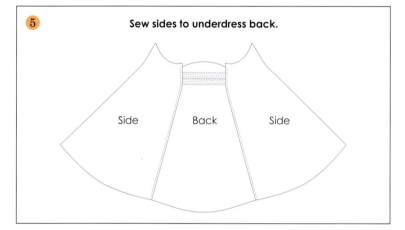

5 Sew sides to underdress back.

Side   Back   Side

Sew the Underdress

1 Finish the bottom edge of the back-facing piece. Stitch the facing piece to the underdress back along the top edge only.

2 Turn the facing inside, press, and edgestitch at ⅛ inch (3 mm). If you want to embellish the exposed back underdress piece with ruffles, do so now (page 113). Note that you'll be stitching elastic casings across this piece in a later step, so space the trims if necessary.

3 Sew three parallel lines across the upper back, as shown at top right, through both layers. Space the lines ¾ inch (2 cm) apart to accommodate the elastic. This forms two casings between the back facing and the back underdress.

4 Cut two pieces of elastic the length of the casings, plus 1 inch (2.5 cm). Working with a safety pin or bodkin, insert a piece of elastic into each casing. Secure the elastic strips at one end, within the overdress seam allowance, with a straight stitch. Cinch the fabric to about two-thirds of its full width, and pin the free ends of the elastics. Sew these ends to the seam allowance as before. Trim the excess elastic.

5 Pin the underdress side pieces to the underdress back piece. The upper edges of the side pieces should extend above the edge of the underdress back piece by the width of the seam allowance. Sew the underdress side pieces to the back piece. Press the seam allowances toward the sides and topstitch at ⅛ inch (3 mm).

6 Sew the underdress front to the sides. Press the seam allowances toward the front and topstitch at ⅛ inch (3 mm).

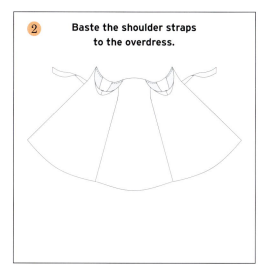

② Baste the shoulder straps to the overdress.

③ Sew the overdress and underdress together along the upper edge, catching the shoulder straps.

Shoulder strap

Overdress

Overdress

Underdress

Join the Dress Layers and Attach the Shoulder Straps

1 (If you're making a skirt version of Feliz, skip to step 3.) Sew the shoulder-strap fronts and backs and strap-facing fronts and backs at the shoulder seams. Press the seam allowances open and topstitch both sides. Sew the shoulder straps to the strap facings along the long edges. Turn the shoulder straps right side out, press, and edgestitch the lengthwise edges at ⅛ inch (3 mm).

2 Pin the front ends of the shoulder straps to the overdress piece, aligning the strap ends with the raw edge of the overdress and positioning the straps at the marks. Repeat for the back strap ends. Baste the straps to the overdress.

3 Turn the underdress inside out. Wrap the overdress/strap unit around the underdress, overdress right side against underdress wrong side. Align the vertical seams and the upper edges of the dresses, and pin along the top edge. Sew this seam, trim the seam allowances, and turn the entire dress right side out. Press the upper edge and topstitch at ⅛ inch (3 mm).

tip!

To make it easier to get all the straps and layers assembled with right sides facing out on the finished garment—as they should be!—I recommend pinning or basting the layers in place first. If you do, you can easily check that everything is lined up properly before you sew the final seams.

Sew the Sash Casings, and Finish

1 Pull the sash ends out the back of the dress, between the under- and overlayers, and pin in place between the marked sash-casing lines. Topstitch along the marked lines, through both layers, taking care not to catch the sash in the stitching. This stitching forms the sash casing and joins the dress bodice layers together.

2 If you're using buttons, mark their placement opposite the button loops. Sew on the buttons.

3 Fold the underdress hem allowance under twice, press, and topstitch.

① Sew the sash casings through the overdress and underdress side layers.

Back   Side   Front

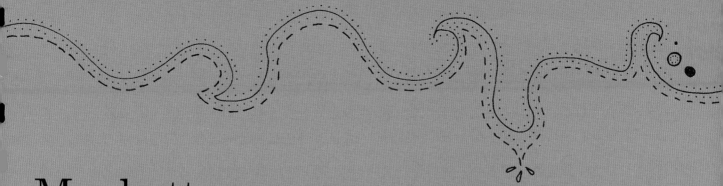

Manhattan Special Occasion Dress

This lovely dress is named for two great towns that bear the name. If you draw a line west from Central Park in Manhattan, New York, to the Pacific Ocean, you'll land in the Los Angeles oceanfront city, Manhattan Beach. The curving separations of the skirt gores allude to ocean waves. The easy slip-on style will take your little one from gathering seashells on the beach to eating pretty parfaits with Grandmother at Tavern on the Green.

The Manhattan dress has a corset-style bodice, cap sleeves, and an integrated underskirt—and because the dress is constructed with a full lining, you can make it reversible if ou like. Notice the hemline sweeps a bit longer in the back. You can bunch and stitch the overdress a bit in the back to create a bustle effect. For fit and fancy, the bodice laces up, either at the back or at both sides.

Recommended Fabrics:

- cotton percale, baby-wale corduroy, velvet, velveteen, batiste, voile, linen, taffeta, lightweight denim, and chambray; heavy overdress fabric needs a lightweight lining.

Notions

- ⅜-inch (1 cm)-wide elastic, about 18 inches (45.7 cm) long
- ribbon for lacing loops, 3 inches (7.5 cm) per loop
- ribbon for cinching, 1¾ yards (1.6 meters) per cinch
- fusible interfacing
- sewing thread

Pattern Piece Cutting List: Pattern Sheet 4

- (A) Bodice center-front piece: Cut two on the fold—one each from shell and from lining fabrics.
- (B) Bodice side-front piece: Cut four—two each from shell and lining fabrics.
- (C) Bodice lower-side back piece: Cut four—two each from shell and lining fabrics.
- (D) Bodice lower-center back piece: Cut two on the fold—one each from shell and lining fabrics.
- (E) Bodice upper-center back piece: Cut two on the fold—one each from shell and lining fabrics.
- (F) Bodice upper-side back piece: Cut four—two each from shell and lining fabrics.
- (G) Bodice front shoulder piece: Cut four—two each from shell and lining fabrics.
- (H) Cap sleeve: Cut four—two each from shell and lining fabrics.
- (I) Collar: Cut two on the fold—one each from shell and lining fabrics.
- (J) Skirt upper-front piece: Cut two on the fold—one each from shell and lining fabrics.
- (K) Skirt upper-side piece: Cut four—two each from shell and lining fabrics.
- (L) Skirt upper-back piece: Cut two on the fold—one each from shell and lining fabrics.
- (M) Skirt lower piece (front, back, and sides): Cut eight on the fold—four each from shell and lining fabrics.

Sewing Manhattan

Begin by sketching your design (page 52). Indicate where various fabrics and trims should be placed, and choose either back or side lacing. Select the appropriate pattern pieces for your garment, and trace them if desired (page 36). Lay the pieces on the fabric and cut them (page 45), then transfer all the marks from the pattern to the fabric.

tip!

Some pattern pieces look similar; others look the same upside-down. To avoid confusion, label the garment pieces and the corresponding lining pieces: "A-1" and "A-2," for example. Lay the pieces flat in their final positions. Or if you've made a kinderquin (page 43), pin them to the form.

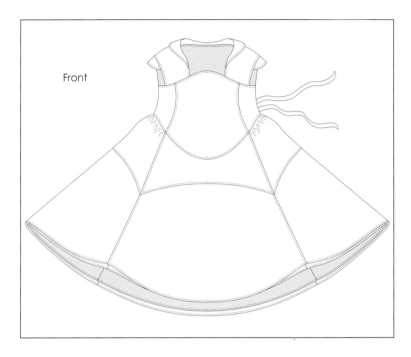

Front

Size Chart

Size	18 mos.–2T 86/92		3T–4T 98/104		5T–6 110/116		7–8 122/128		9–10 134/140		11–12 146/152	
	US	EURO	US	EURO	US	EURO	US	EURO	US	EURO	US	EURO
Chest	26"	66 cm	26¾"	68 cm	27½"	70 cm	29⅛"	74 cm	30¾"	78 cm	33⅞"	86 cm
Shoulder Width	3"	7.5 cm	3⅛"	8 cm	3⅜"	8.5 cm	3½"	9 cm	3¾"	9.5 cm	4⅛"	10.5 cm
Front Length	23¼"	59 cm	26"	66 cm	28¾"	73 cm	32¼"	82 cm	35⅞"	91 cm	40⅛"	102 cm

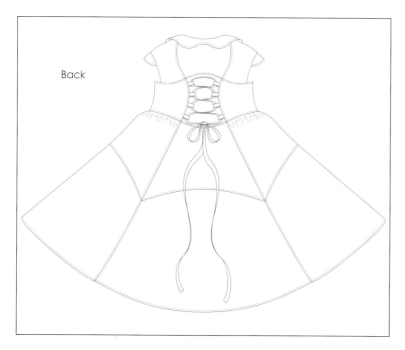

Back

note: *Sew all seams with right sides together, unless otherwise indicated. For construction seams and topstitching, use a straight stitch. Because the dress is fully lined, it's not necessary to finish all the seam allowances on the bodice. The skirt layers are separate, however, so you may choose to overlock or zigzag those allowances. Unless otherwise indicated, topstitch through the garment and all layers of the seam allowances, ⅛ inch (3 mm) or ¼ inch (6 mm) from the seamline. For basting, use a straight stitch set for a long stitch length. Remove basting stitches after sewing the final seam.*

Fabric Requirements Table

Size	Fabric Width	18 mos.–2T 86/92		3T–4T 98/104		5T–6 110/116		7–8 122/128		9–10 134/140		11–12 146/152	
		US	EURO	US	EURO	US	EURO	US	EURO	US	EURO	US	EURO
Dress	54" (140 cm)	3 yd	2.7 m	3¼ yd	2.9 m	3⅜ yd	3 m	3⅜ yd	3.1 cm	6 yd	5.6 m	7 yd	6.4 m

Amount required to make the entire garment in one fabric.

Sew the Bodice

1   Sew the bodice center-front piece (A) to the bodice side-front pieces (B). If you want to cinch the dress at the sides, insert ribbon loops into these seams, as described in the sidebar at left. Press the seam allowances toward the center front. If you have added ribbon loops, do not topstitch. If you omitted the loops, topstitch these seams at ⅛ inch (3 mm). Repeat for the corresponding lining pieces, omitting the ribbon loops.

RIBBON LOOPS

To make even ribbon loops for the side or back lacing, cut a piece of ribbon the length of the seam where the loops will go. Mark the ribbon at equal intervals to indicate the loop placement. A simple way to ensure equal intervals is to fold the ribbon in half, mark the center, then fold each half in half and mark the center again. Fold as many times as needed for the desired number of loops. Cut short lengths of ribbon—about 2½ inches (6.5 cm) long—and fold each piece in half to form a loop. Pin a loop to the ribbon at each mark and sew along the ribbon to secure all the loops. Insert this ribbon-with-loops unit into the seam as you sew, with the loops facing away from the raw edge.

Sew ribbon loops to a length of ribbon first.

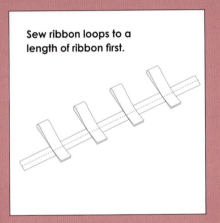

Insert the ribbon with loops into the seam.

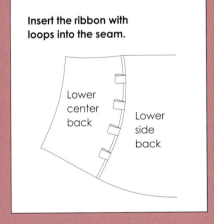

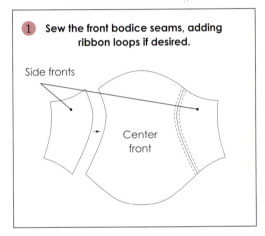

1 Sew the front bodice seams, adding ribbon loops if desired.

Side fronts

Center front

2   If you want to embellish the bodice lower-center back piece (D) with trims, do so now; this way, you can catch the trim ends in the vertical seams. Then, sew the bodice lower-center back to the bodice lower-side back pieces (C). Insert ribbon loops in these seam, as described in the sidebar. Press the seam allowances toward the sides, but do not topstitch. Repeat for the corresponding lining pieces, omitting the ribbon loops.

3 Sew the bodice upper-center back piece (E) to the bodice upper-side back pieces (F). Press these seam allowances toward the sides and topstitch at ⅛ inch (3 mm). Repeat for the corresponding lining pieces.

4 Sew the upper-back bodice to the lower-back bodice, aligning the center/side vertical seams. Press the seam allowances upward and topstitch at ⅛ inch (3 mm). Repeat for the corresponding lining pieces.

5 Sew the front-shoulder pieces (G) to the upper edge of the back bodice. Align the inner edges of the shoulder pieces with the bodice center/side seams. Press the seam allowances toward the shoulders and topstitch. Repeat for the corresponding lining pieces.

6 Sew the bodice front to the bodice back at the side seams. Repeat for the corresponding lining pieces.

tip!

Manhattan is a fully lined dress, so the lining must fit the outer dress perfectly. That's easiest to accomplish if you sew one seam of the shell, then sew the corresponding seam of the lining. As you work, compare lining to shell. Make any fitting adjustments to both pieces at the same time, and the shell will fit the lining like a glove.

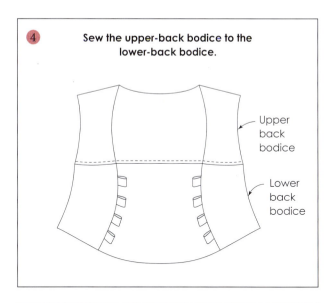

④ Sew the upper-back bodice to the lower-back bodice.

Upper back bodice

Lower back bodice

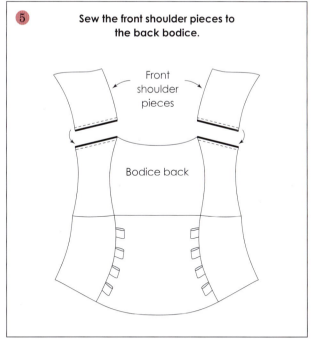

⑤ Sew the front shoulder pieces to the back bodice.

Front shoulder pieces

Bodice back

Prepare the Collar and Cap Sleeves

1 Apply fusible interfacing to the shell and lining collar pieces (I).

2 Sew the two collar pieces together along the outer (longer) edge. Trim and notch this seam allowance. Turn the collar right side out and press. Edgestitch the outer edge at ⅛ inch (3 mm).

3 Sew the cap sleeve shell and lining pieces (H) along the round, outer edge. Turn the cap sleeves right side out and press. Edgestitch along the outer edge of the cap sleeve at ⅛ inch (3 mm)

4 Pin the collar to the bodice shell neckline, matching the collar center with the back bodice center, collar lining side against the shell right side. Baste the collar to the bodice along the seamline.

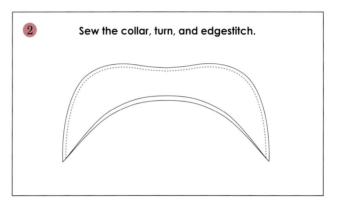

② Sew the collar, turn, and edgestitch.

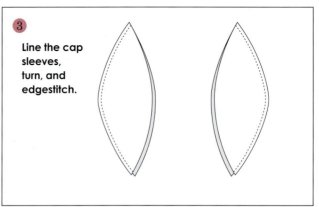

③ Line the cap sleeves, turn, and edgestitch.

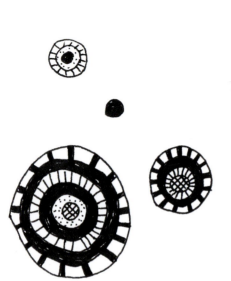

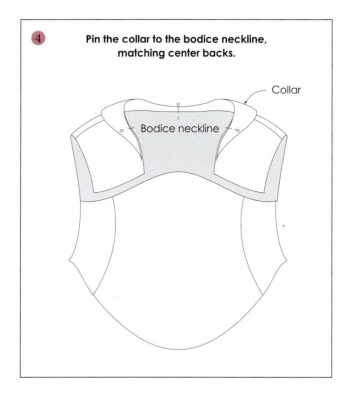

④ Pin the collar to the bodice neckline, matching center backs.

Collar

Bodice neckline

Attach the Bodice Lining to the Bodice Shell

1 Pin the bodice lining and shell right sides together along the back neckline and inner edges of the front shoulder pieces. The collar is sandwiched between the shell and lining layers.

2 Sew the lining to the shell as pinned, securing the collar in this line of stitching. Turn the bodice right side out and press. Topstitch at ⅛ inch (3 mm).

3 Pin the prepared cap sleeves to the shell shoulder at the marks, with the sleeve open edges aligned with the shoulder raw edge, and the sleeve mark aligned on the shoulder seam. Keep the lining free. Baste the cap sleeves to the shell at the seamline.

4 Turn the garment inside out and align the shell and lining armhole seams, right sides together, sandwiching the cap sleeves between the layers, and pin. Sew these seams, catching the cap sleeve in the stitching.

5 Turn the shoulders right side out and press.

6 Separate the bodice shell and lining, turning both inside out. Bring the shoulder pieces toward the front and pin the free edges of the shoulder pieces to the front bodice shell, right sides together, between the mark and the front center/side seam.

7 Baste the shoulder pieces to the bodice shell as pinned. Turn your work right side out and have a quick fitting: Make sure the child's head fits through the neck opening and that the neckline isn't too low. Adjust if necessary. Turn the work inside-out again.

8 When the shoulders are satisfactorily fitted, pin the bodice shell to the bodice lining, right sides together, from the underarm and across the front neckline to the other underarm. The shoulder pieces are enclosed between the front bodice layers. Sew this seam, trim and clip as needed, and turn the bodice right side out.

1 Pin the bodice and lining along the armhole edges with the collar between the layers.

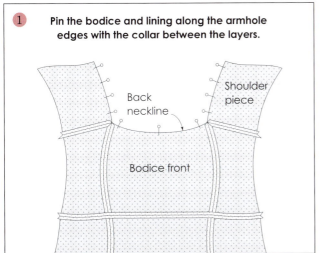

Back neckline

Shoulder piece

Bodice front

4 Sew the bodice and lining along the armhole edges.

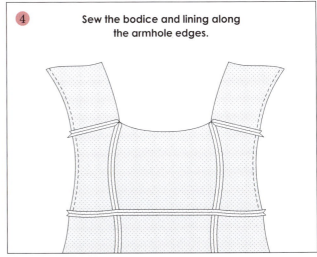

2 Sew lining to shell, then turn the bodice right-side-out.

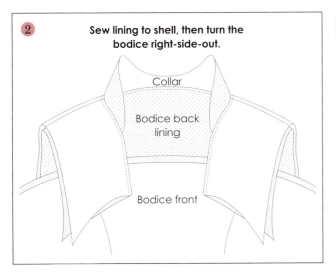

Collar

Bodice back lining

Bodice front

5 Turn the shoulders right-side-out and press.

Completed shoulder pieces and cap sleeves

3 Baste the cap sleeve to the bodice shell armhole.

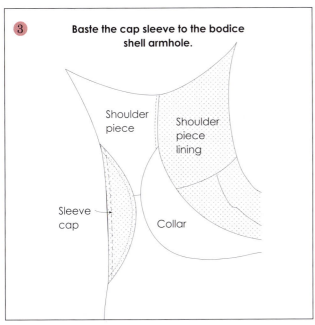

Shoulder piece

Shoulder piece lining

Sleeve cap

Collar

6 Pin the shoulder pieces to the front bodice shell.

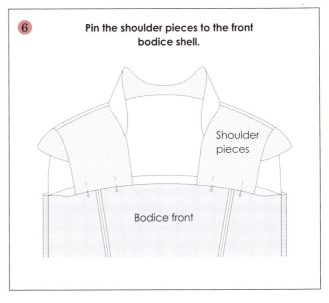

Shoulder pieces

Bodice front

9   Topstitch the armholes and front neckline at ⅛ inch (3 mm), in a continuous line of stitching, as shown in the drawing.

10   Add elastic to the back bodice if desired, as described below. The bodice is now complete. If you're making a corset top, hem it by folding the lower edge under twice and topstitching. Alternatively, you can add a binding along the hem edge. If you're making a dress, continue as follows.

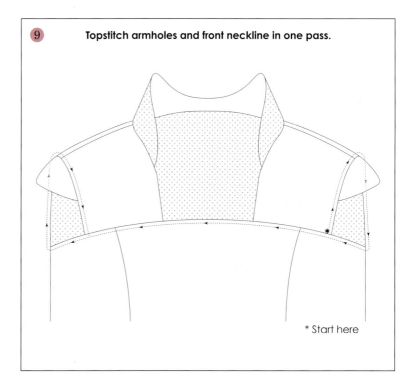

9   **Topstitch armholes and front neckline in one pass.**

* Start here

FINE-TUNE THE FIT

You may want to insert elastic into the back bodice for a better fit.

Step 1. With a marking tool, mark four parallel, horizontal lines across the lower-center back panel, spaced ½ inch (1.3 cm) apart, to form three casings that can accommodate ⅜-inch (1 cm)-wide elastic.

Step 2. Pin the lower-back bodice lining and shell layers together. Stitch along the marked lines, through the shell and lining layers, creating the casings for the elastic.

Step 3. Cut three pieces of elastic, 2 to 3 inches (5 to 7 cm) longer than the casings. Insert the elastics into the casings, working with a safety pin or bodkin. Pin one end of the elastics along one center/side back seam.

Step 4. Topstitch the center/side back seam, catching in the ends of the elastics. Cinch the elastics to reduce the bodice back panel to about 70 percent of its original width, and pin the free ends along the opposite center/side seam. Topstitch this seam to secure these elastic ends. Reach between the bodice layers and trim the excess elastic.

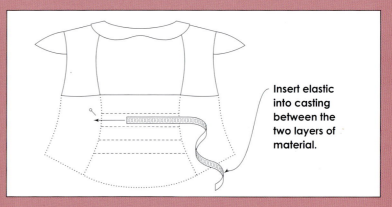

Insert elastic into casting between the two layers of material.

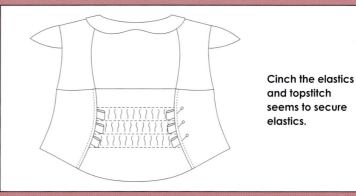

Cinch the elastics and topstitch seems to secure elastics.

Sew the Skirt

1 Sew the skirt upper-front shell piece (J) to one skirt lower shell piece (M). Press up the seam allowance and topstitch at ⅛ inch (3 mm). Repeat for the corresponding lining pieces.

2 Sew the skirt upper-side shell pieces (K) to two skirt lower shell pieces (M). Press up the seam allowance and topstitch. Repeat for the corresponding lining pieces.

3 Sew the skirt upper-back shell piece (L) to one skirt lower shell piece (M). Press up the seam allowance and topstitch. Repeat for the corresponding lining pieces.

4 Sew the skirt side panels to the skirt back panel; then sew the skirt front panel to the side panels. Press the seam allowances away from the side panel and topstitch. Repeat for the lining pieces.

5 Sew two lines of gathering stitches along the top edges of the skirt side pieces, where marked. Pull the bobbin thread gently to gather the side panels to fit the bodice sides. Repeat for the skirt lining.

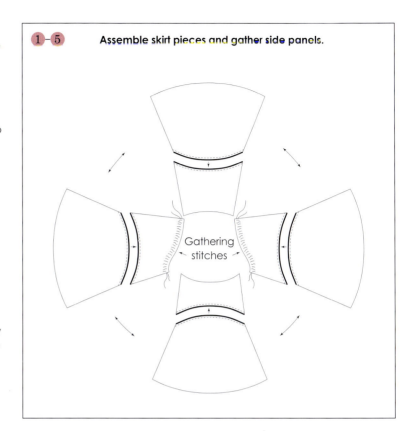

1–5 Assemble skirt pieces and gather side panels.

Gathering stitches

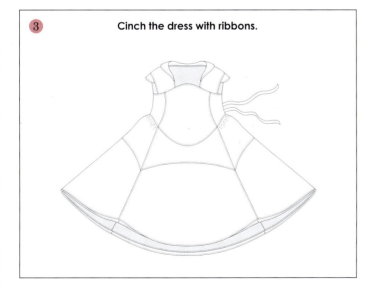

3 Cinch the dress with ribbons.

Attach the Skirt to the Bodice and Finish

1 Pin the skirt shell to the bodice shell, aligning the skirt upper edge with the bodice lower edge, and matching the skirt seams to the bodice center/side seams. Adjust the gathers to fit. Sew this waistline seam, press the seam allowances up, and topstitch. Repeat for the bodice lining and lining skirt.

2 Fold the skirt shell hem up twice, press, and topstitch. Repeat for the lining skirt.

3 Cut ribbons for the side or back lacings, approximately 5 ft (1.5 m) per ribbon. Lace the ribbons through the ribbon loops and tie.

• *Petal ruching is a soft, scalloped frill that adds dimension and interest. Embroidery designs by Nicole Hildebrandt.*

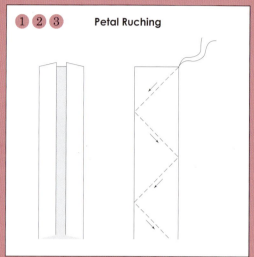

Petal Ruching

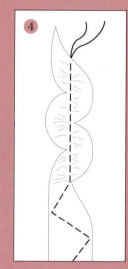

PETAL RUCHING

Unlike the ruching on page 76, which is gathered at its center, petal ruching has gathering stitches that follow a zigzag course back and forth from edge to edge. When the stitches are pulled up, the edges scallop. This technique creates a beautiful, simple "how-did-you-do-that?" embellishment. Petal ruching is especially pretty if you begin with a bias strip of fabric that is cut wide enough for you to fold the long edges to the middle, which will put the scallop "petals" on the folds.

Step 1: Cut a bias strip of fabric approximately 3 inches (7.5 cm) wide and about three times as long as the desired finished length. Place it wrong side up on your ironing board. Fold both long edges so they meet in the middle and press, as shown above. This is the wrong side of the ruche.

Step 2: Place the strip on your worktable right side up. Using a washable marker, draw a zigzag guideline across the strip at 45 degrees to the long edges (the line is on the straight grain of the fabric).

Step 3. Sew a line of gathering stitches along the marked guideline, stopping with the needle down each time you reach the edge, lifting the foot, and pivoting the fabric. (As a shortcut, I mark just the first diagonal line from one long edge to the other. I sew along that line and, at the end, rotate the strip so that the stitching is parallel to the horizontal marks on the needle plate of my machine and sew the next line.

Step 4: Starting at one end, gently pull the bobbin thread to gather the strip—the petals form along the edges. Take care not to break the thread.

Step 5: Pin the ruche in place. Adjust the gathers gently so the petals appear uniform.

Step 6: To attach the ruche, sew along the center, over the gathering stitches, with a straight stitch.

• Elegant and sophisticated, these embroidered roses are very easy to make. They're not just for dresses: adding ribbon roses to jeans or T-shirts will take the everyday to the runway.

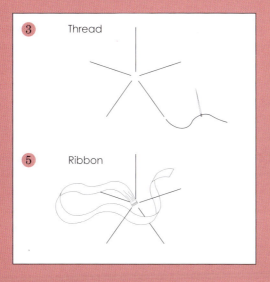

EMBROIDERED RIBBON ROSES

These pretty roses are made with ribbon or with strips of sheer fabric (such as net, tulle, chiffon, or even voile). If you use fabric, the edges may ravel a bit, which can be appealing. It may be easier to embroider these if you use a hoop, but you can embroider without one.

Step 1: If appropriate, interface your base fabric before you begin (see "Appliqué" step 4 on page 71).

Step 2: If using fabric for the rose, cut a strip approximately 1 inch (2.5 cm) wide and about 20 inches (50 cm) long. If using ribbon, cut a piece this same length.

Step 3: Thread a needle with thread that matches the fabric strip or ribbon (or use invisible thread). Referring to the top of the drawing above, sew five loose, large stitches in a starfish pattern in your base fabric. Make each stitch approximately 1¼ inches (3 cm) long. (If you're using narrow ribbon, make the starfish stitches shorter. Experiment to find a proportion that's right for your ribbon.)

Step 4: Tack one end of the fabric strip to the center of the starfish stitches. (If you are using embroidery ribbon, thread it into another needle and bring it up through the fabric directly.) Leave the threaded needle attached to the base fabric.

Step 5: Referring to the bottom of the drawing, weave the fabric strip over and under, over and under the five arms of the thread starfish, around and around. As you weave, the strip will twist, which is perfectly fine. The twisting will lend the appearance of opening rose petals. It's easier to weave if you put the strip in a bodkin or attach it to a safety pin.

Step 6: Tuck the end of the strip under the rose. With the threaded needle, tack the edges of the rose in place.

Index

Have I said enough? Have I said too much? Did you learn something new? Were you inspired just a bit? Is there a pretty little girl you know dancing around in her new, handmade outfit? Is there a dashing young man exclaiming, "Thanks, Mom!"? Did you have fun? Was there sewing, clothes, kids, and love? I really and truly hope so. I hope you will tell me about your experiences sewing these designs and sewing for that special little someone.